ANXIOUS ATTACHMENT NO MORE !!!

THE EXCLUSIVE ROADMAP TO STRIVE TOWARDS SECURE ATTACHMENT IN RELATIONSHIPS

TAHA ZAID

CONTENTS

Introduction … 7

1. Understanding Reactive Attachment Disorder and Insecure Attachment in Adulthood … 15
2. The Remarkable Patterns in Dating Someone with an Anxious Attachment Style … 32
3. How Secure Style Differs from Anxious Attachment … 45
4. Your Brain and Relationships … 58
5. Strive Towards Secure Attachment Style … 70
6. The Ultimate Dating Exercises … 83
7. Reforming Your Attachment Style … 95
8. The Self Esteem, Intimacy, Autonomy Shortcut … 109

Conclusion … 129
References … 133

© Copyright 2021 - All rights reserved.

The content contained within this book may not be reproduced, duplicated or transmitted without direct written permission from the author or the publisher.

Under no circumstances will any blame or legal responsibility be held against the publisher, or author, for any damages, reparation, or monetary loss due to the information contained within this book. Either directly or indirectly. You are responsible for your own choices, actions, and results.

Legal Notice:

This book is copyright protected. This book is only for personal use. You cannot amend, distribute, sell, use, quote or paraphrase any part, or the content within this book, without the consent of the author or publisher.

Disclaimer Notice:

Please note the information contained within this document is for educational and entertainment purposes only. All effort has been executed to present accurate, up to date, and reliable, complete information. No warranties of any kind are declared or implied. Readers acknowledge that the author is not engaging in the rendering of legal, financial, medical or professional advice. The content within this book has been derived from various sources. Please consult a licensed professional before attempting any techniques outlined in this book.

By reading this document, the reader agrees that under no circumstances is the author responsible for any losses, direct or indirect, which are incurred as a result of the use of the information contained within this document, including, but not limited to errors, omissions, or inaccuracies.

SECURELY ATTACHED BOOTCAMP

The Exclusive Journey To Strive Towards Secure Attachment

What we are offering :

- **Free PDF** of "**The Attachment-Styles Mastery Book**" To Acquire The Right Skills And Adopt The Solid Foundations Of The Attachment Theory.
- **Free Weekly Resources & Chat Consultation** For My Exclusive Members.
- **Free & Early Copy** Of All My Next Releases.

Join The Facebook Community, And Speed Up Your Healing Journey...

SCAN THE QR CODE TO JOIN THE
EXCLUSIVE COMMUNITY

FB Group: Securely Attached Bootcamp

INTRODUCTION

Of the global adult population, twenty percent of people have an anxious attachment style, meaning that one-fifth of all humans yearn to have romantic intimacy. Yet, they still struggle to have the relationships they want because of their recurring concerns. For those who have anxiety in relationships, their attachment style causes them to doubt their partners' devotion. They often become convinced that they can never be good enough for their partner's love. These insecurities create small cracks in relationships and put distance between couples. As a result, relationship anxiety often debilitates couples, making it hard for individuals to enter into healthy relationships without self-sabotage or intense worry.

Anxiety around relationships is common, and everyone faces that anxiety at some point, but people with anxious attachments persistently have doubts about their relationships. One study led by the American Addiction Centers discovered that among their respondents, the top insecurity subjects reported that they felt their partner didn't think they were good enough. Over one-third of people in the study had this concern. The following two main concerns people had was that their partner was cheating on them, regardless of actual evidence of infidelity, and that their partner did not find them attractive. These concerns all point to insecure attachment and relationship anxiety, and they are all ubiquitous. Further, they make it hard to maintain trust between partners. Thus, while these doubts may seem small, especially if you keep them to yourself, they can grow much larger when you don't appropriately acknowledge them and understand the damage they can cause.

Unfortunately, anxious attachment doesn't just harm your relationships. It hurts your very ability to feel confident and worthy. People who have an anxious attachment style tend to have lower self-esteem. They also have an increased risk for mental illnesses, like anxiety disorders or depression. Anxious attachment ripples through your life, and those ripples can make you feel unsteady and unable to ever feel truly safe in your environment or any environment.

Much of the mental hardship associated with insecure attachment stems from childhood. When a child doesn't feel like their caregivers give them the safety and encouragement that they crave, it's natural that they'll grow up and feel like they weren't good enough or that people will never love them. The hurts of their past continue to fester, and it's hard to move on from trauma and past pain without understanding the mechanics of attachment.

When you have relationship anxiety, you cannot be fully present in your relationship. You end up wasting time worrying about what might go wrong rather than spending quality time with your partner. As a result, anxiety can make you and your partner more distant from each other. That distance can result in increased relationship troubles, which eventually can lead to the relationship's complete disintegration. In essence, by fearing that your partner will not love you enough and listening to your insecurities, you push your partner away before they can push you away. Thus, an anxious attachment style can cause you to bring to life the very situation you were afraid would happen.

Think of all the ways your life would change if you put your anxiety to bed. Imagine closing the distance all your worries create. Your relationships will instantly change because you and your partner will be able to establish a new level of trust, compassion, and intimacy. You will start to be more mindful in your relationship, and you will have the mental clarity to let the other person into your private world. You will still have some doubts because doubts are a natural part of your cognitive process, but they will be fleeting. You'll learn to let your doubts exist without taking them too seriously. When you can push past the fear of getting hurt, your anxious thoughts will no longer be ropes binding you to illogical thought processes.

Ultimately, your anxiety does not come from a place of rationality; instead, it comes from an instinctual urge to protect yourself from the dangers that have previously harmed you. Your fears are not invalid; you have them for a reason, but when they start to make you feel like you cannot move forward, that's when you need to make a change.

Improving your attachment style often feels like a losing battle. You think, "I'm stuck in my ways. I will never change." Still, emerging research published by the Journal of Personality and Social Psychology has shown that while changing your attachment style takes effort and self-awareness, it is possible. It isn't as difficult as people think. Moreover, the same research has shown that the study participants shifted their attachment style and became more content about their relationships. No matter how anxious you are about your relationship, you are not a lost cause, and there is always hope for improvement.

All you have to do to create relationship success is to be willing to invest the time and energy into making small incremental changes. You don't need to have instant improvement, and you shouldn't expect that. It takes time to retrain your brain and convince yourself that you are secure in your relationship.

As you continue reading, you will learn about the central concepts related to attachment theory. You'll learn about Reactive Attachment Disorder and the differences between secure relationships and insecure ones. Further, you will discover the trends people with anxious attachment have when dating and how to lessen those patterns' impacts. I will also tell you how your nervous system plays a role in your relationships. Don't worry; all the neuroscience in this book is explained in concise and fundamental terms that anyone can understand. Each of these ideas will give you a strong foundation for the methods you will use to change your attachment style.

In the second half of the book, once I have established the necessary background, you will learn techniques to improve your attachment. I will show you the steps you can use to develop a secure attachment style, including scientific methods and psychological processes. Several dating exercises will help you practice the strategies to feel confident as you try to create new relationships or maintain current ones. Finally, I will provide a cohesive roadmap, which will help you form essential tenets to help you resist any lingering anxious thoughts you have. You will learn about the roles of self-esteem, intimacy, and autonomy in your relationships.

The changes in your life won't change the minute you close this book, but you will start to feel a mental transition as you begin to apply the healing technique provided in this book. Your old ways will take time and effort to change, but if you commit to the methods outlined here, you will see improvement, and you will learn to manage the worries that paralyze you and prevent you from moving forward with relationships. I have applied these changes to myself, and despite my initial doubts, I have learned how transformative they can be.

For years, I struggled to maintain relationships that made me feel secure. I went into relationships with the best intentions, but I was always in panic mode, feeling sure that something was dreadfully wrong. I assumed my partner could never love me enough, and when my partner tried to reassure me, I never believed in the assurances. Relationships that could have been great became sources of great anxiety. I'd stay up at night worrying about my partner, realizing that I wasn't the person I seemed to be. Maintaining relationships was a challenge that I never thought I'd handle, and that was a mindset that caused me great despair. I tried to change my habits, but I always wound up repeating the same mistakes. I'd self-sabotage and start to pull away from my partner discreetly and unconsciously before things could get too serious. After all, serious meant a more significant potential for danger.

Not only did my romantic relationships suffer, but the more I worried about my romantic relationships, the more I worried about my other relationships. I doubted that anyone could like me as I was, and I assumed that my friends were only hanging out with me because they were loyal or friendly. As all the doubts added up, my self-esteem reached an all-time low. My relationship anxiety brought out the worst parts of myself. I felt depressed and on edge. My moods were all over the place, and I behaved in a way that wasn't normal for me. When I wasn't in relationships, my doubts retreated just a little, taking a recess as I regrouped, but each time I began dating again, my head went into overdrive. I didn't know how to make myself better while still maintaining a romantic life. I wondered many times if there was a chance I'd never have both romance and happiness.

Before I learned about anxious attachment, I thought there was something inherently wrong with me. I was empowered as I began studying the psychological reasons behind my relationship woes. To understand my relationship fears and those of millions of people like me, I dove into research and compiled findings from the experts in the field and read compelling stories of those who have resisted their anxious attachments, and learned to create more secure relationships. Armed with an understanding of why my relationships were tense and comforted by stories of people like me, I began to address the outstanding issues contributing to my worry. It is the mix of cohesive facts and human experience that perfectly combines the scientific with the emotional.

Countless people I've encountered have had similar stories to mine, and each time I find someone who shares in the feelings that once dominated my life, I no longer feel like those feelings made me an outcast, unlovable, or bound to be unhappy. Maybe you relate to some of the things I have experienced and feel a similar drive to create change. The answer is in educating yourself on anxious attachment and all the principles related to it.

While humans have uncovered so many elements of attachment, we always have more to discover. Fortunately, the attachment theory has developed tremendously since psychoanalyst John Bowlby first noted it during the mid-twentieth century. Many of the main ideas and principles will be outlined in the chapters to come. There's still so much for researchers to uncover about attachment styles and how to make people feel more secure in their relationships, and the research continues to evolve. Therefore, I urge you to dive in and learn as much as possible about this topic. While psychologists are still figuring out attachment theory's details, they are confident in several ideas about attachment, which you can use to improve your relationships. These methods are ones that I have used, as have many others who have changed their attachment styles.

When you always feel anxious in a relationship, it becomes arduous to deal with your partner, and your anxiety can also increase your partner's anxiety if they have it. As a result, addressing the anxiety you have in relationships is one of the best things that you can do to take back your life. Every day you don't manage your anxious attachment, you are straining any relationships you have. You are delaying the happiness you could feel, so it's time to stop feeling hopeless about your situation and start making a change.

1

UNDERSTANDING REACTIVE ATTACHMENT DISORDER AND INSECURE ATTACHMENT IN ADULTHOOD

Attachment theory states responses like crying and clinging to parents are evolutionary, and they help ensure a child's safety, and therefore, they help the survival of the human species. When a child is cared for, they can more easily survive because they can cry out to their parents and their parents will fulfill their needs. Those instincts have continued throughout the generations and have become an essential part of our sense of safety, even in adulthood. Your relationship style often dictates how you interact in all relationships. When you have an insecure attachment style, you may respond differently to stress and worry in relationships than those with a secure attachment style. People form their attachment style in childhood, but they often continue well into adulthood.

Children are born unable to care for their own needs; thus, they rely on their primary caregivers to attend to those needs and ensure that they are safe and secure. These early relationships with their caregivers create an expectation for children regarding attachment because a child's primary caregivers, usually their parents, establish whether children will feel psychologically and physiologically secure. Each child needs reliable and quick care to feel protected, and they don't just need care for their physical needs, but they also need care for emotional needs, such as comfort, nurturing, and positive attention. When a caretaker meets a child's needs, the child can have a secure attachment. When the parent does not meet the child's needs, the child may develop attachment issues or a full-blown attachment disorder.

Specifically, when one exposes a child to an environment that does not make them feel secure or appropriately cared for, they may develop an attachment disorder that can have long-term consequences to their ability to form and maintain relationships, including romantic relationships. This condition is called Reactive Attachment Disorder (RAD). RAD is not a common condition, but it represents one of the extremes resulting when a child can't form secure attachments during the first several years of their lives. Circumstances like physical, emotional, or sexual abuse are all examples of actions that can lead to RAD, but other factors may play a role. While clinicians don't often diagnose RAD, understanding this condition highlights some of the symptoms and causes that show how attachment issues can persist into adulthood and result in anxious relationships.

Kids who have RAD tend to display similar symptoms, although the condition is always unique to each individual who has it. These children tend not to seek out care when they feel upset, and they may not respond appropriately when they do get comfort. Further, they may grow to be more moody, irritable, or anxious without explanation. RAD children may also cry more often and seem depressed. Children with RAD may have worse social outcomes because they may not be interested in spending time with other children or loved ones. They may also not understand how to connect with their peers appropriately, and they may not make eye contact or make other common social gestures. This condition not only impacts their social functioning, but it can lead to cognitive issues and hyperactive behavior. These children often resort to self-soothing mechanisms, such as rocking themselves or other repetitive motions due to their lack of security and comfort from caregivers.

Because RAD is, for the most part, only diagnosed among children between the ages of nine months and five years (although clinicians can diagnose as long as symptoms appear before the age of five with a duration of at least one year), people may experience this condition and its symptoms while never having it diagnosed. Often, the attachment issues caused by RAD are unknown until later in life. Thus, clinicians do not attribute attachment disorders to adults. However, clinicians may still recognize untreated attachment issues among adults who seek treatment for other correlated problems such as anxiety, depression, or relationship problems. Further, with increased awareness about secure and insecure attachment, parents, child welfare professionals, and other caregivers can better prevent and treat attachment issues before becoming too severe and before children reach adulthood.

Untreated attachment issues can be incredibly harmful. As children grow up and start to mature, they may face more complex issues because of their RAD (or other attachment problems). For example, studies show that children with RAD are more prone to adverse outcomes such as a hard time controlling their anger and issues at school. They may also use unhealthy coping mechanisms to cope with their insecure attachment, which can take the form of mental health conditions, such as anxiety, depression, substance abuse, and eating disorders. Thus, attachment issues profoundly impact a person's ability to function and interact with others in satisfying ways, which is why, no matter the level of severity, you need to address your insecure attachment. Still, before you learn how to manage your anxious attachment, you need to understand what causes it and how it impacts you in your daily life and how it impacts your relationships.

Causes of Insecure Attachment

The causes of insecure attachment are multifaceted, so there's no single factor that causes RAD. It is often associated with abusive childhoods, but even children who have highly abusive and uncaring early childhoods may not ever experience this disorder. That doesn't mean the trauma impacts them any less adversely. Still, it means they responded to their trauma in other ways. Researchers aren't fully aware of why some kids may develop insecure attachment. In contrast, others do not, but they have found some patterns that illuminate why insecure attachment occurs. This research shows that disorders like RAD are often the product of several factors occurring at once, which leads to the development of dysfunctional attachment styles.

Genetic factors do play a role in a person's attachment style, but a child can overcome those factors with the right environment, which research suggests is the most crucial factor of attachment. Many studies indicate that when a child has a family history of personality disorders, they will be more likely to have attachment issues. This genetic connection could be indirect because untreated personality disorders can lead to more volatile and insecure homes, a trigger for RAD. Still, there could also be something in children's genetic makeup that makes them directly more susceptible. Thus, while genetic factors are unlikely to account solely for the onset of RAD, they do play a role in whether the disorder will trigger in a child who has other conditional factors that predispose them to an anxious attachment. Genetic factors are important to consider, but the research on these factors still has much growing to do before researchers will have a clearer idea of the genetic power over conditions such as RAD and insecure attachment.

Physical factors also impact the development of insecure attachment. Research has shown that children who experience attachment issues have distinct brain functioning and may experience slowed brain development. Thus, the wiring of a child's brain could determine whether they will develop RAD. The brain's functioning can shift in the face of trauma, and how it shifts to account for the lack of care or bonding with a parent may highlight what physical changes suggest RAD. With more study, this information could help improve diagnosis and treatment for those with attachment issues, but, as with the genetic factors, there's still a long way to go with this research.

Environmental causes are some of the most studied, and they are often considered the most prominent factor of whether a child will develop attachment issues. If a parent physically abuses a child, the child will not feel safe, and they will worry that their parent will hurt them. As they encounter other relationships, they become nervous because they learned that bonding could equal hurt. The same is true of any other type of abuse or insufficient care. A baby whose parents neglect them and force them to sit in a dirty diaper for hours, for instance, is going to learn that they cannot rely on other people, and therefore, they cannot rely on other humans. The human brain is prone to cognitive distortions, which are ideas that people form based on the misinterpretation of circumstances. People commonly create cognitive distortions when they look at information and make an inaccurate generalization. A child who is not cared for by a caregiver will assume that all people won't care for them, even if the thought is subconscious. Thus, they may avoid or become afraid of forming relationships because forming relationships could lead to that perceived danger. A child not getting the care they need reinforces the cognitive distortion, resulting in the long-term impacts RAD sufferers may face, even into adulthood. Thus, the environmental factors are most telling when it comes to developing attachment disorders, but genetic and physical factors also fuel the condition.

There are several risk factors for anxious attachment. For example, a child who grew up alongside another child with RAD is more likely to have an attachment disorder. Those rates are from an estimated sixty-seven to seventy-five percent. Additionally, children who experience institutional living (i.e., a hospital or orphanage) tend to be more prone to attachment issues. Additionally, young children who have unstable placements in homes are also more likely to form an anxious attachment. Hence, children in foster care who switch environments are often more likely to feel insecure, even if their foster parents are loving and nurturing.

Moreover, the type of caregiver is also necessary to note. Teen parents often result in attachment issues, as do mentally ill parents or parents who have substance abuse issues. The same problems exist when a child has a caregiver with an intellectual disability. That is not to say that a child in those caregiving scenarios is bound to struggle with attachment. Still, when a child is in those environments, special care must be given to ensure that they form healthy attachments in those critical years.

Signs of Insecure Attachment

If you or a loved one had undiagnosed or untreated RAD as a child or even subclinical attachment issues, those problems don't vanish when a child becomes an adult. They fester, and they threaten to destroy a person's adult relationships. You may not realize that a problem exists, but the attachment issues may become more apparent upon looking at the symptoms. These signs alone do not suggest insecure attachment. Still, suppose you have several of them and struggle to have healthy, long-lasting relationships. In that case, you may very well have unaddressed attachment issues, or you may recognize these symptoms in someone important to you.

It's probably not a surprise that along with anxious attachment often comes anxiety. This anxiety can grow as the disorder continues, and it can become much more than just relationship anxiety. Someone who experienced insecure attachments may become consistently afraid of certain things beyond abandonment or a lack of care from others. For example, a child whose parent did not adequately feed them may become an adult who is afraid of being hungry. That adult may hoard food, and they may overeat even when they are not hungry simply because they are anxious that they won't be able to eat enough. When identifying attachment issues, you should first determine whether you have anxiety about relationships. Still, you should also see if there are other anxieties related to the inconsistency or absence of care that you have experienced because those fears can also point you towards what you need to repair.

Attachment issues can cause not only anxiety but they can also cause sadness, fear, and moodiness in adults as well as children. When you worry that the people in your life aren't going to love you the way you want them to, it's common to feel emotionally on edge. Your fearful response is your brain's way of trying to keep you safe. Fear keeps you vigilant, and vigilance keeps you alive. As a child, you didn't feel safe, so your brain adapted to ensure you stayed alive. You learned not to trust others and to trust in yourself instead. Then, even when you have found a safe environment, you still have those same old brain patterns that cause you to emotionally react to situations that remind you of when you were a helpless kid. Your emotions will often be complicated and hard to understand, making you lash out and feel like you are on an emotional roller coaster. Still, all of those responses are normal when you have traumatic experiences.

Loneliness is common among adults who had RAD (again, it doesn't matter if you were diagnosed with RAD or not). When you have a hard time forming bonds with other people, you may isolate yourself, and you might not be able to connect with people on a deeper, intimate level. Instead, you will settle for surface-level attachment because it is safer, or you will desperately try to cling to relationships that are bad for you. You'll probably yearn for a deeper connection than that shallow one, but because of your past hurts, you feel emotionally unable to commit that much attention and emotional investment into your relationships with other people. As a result, your relationships suffer, and you never get the love you want or deserve.

Further, if you have an anxious attachment style, you may be attracted to people with avoidant attachment. Avoidants struggle to commit and feed into anxious attachment anxieties; such a relationship can be even more alienating. Accordingly, many people with unhealthy attachment styles feel lonely, and they struggle to maintain relationships that will make them feel fulfilled.

When you have an anxious attachment, you may also have control issues. People who are insecure in relationships may try to dictate how those relationships unfold. They might want to control the other person's behaviors and interests because they are afraid that if they don't assert that control, the other person will leave them or reject them. You may not mean to be controlling, but your insecurities may make you want to force relationships in specific directions so that you feel safe and can give yourself a reprieve from the intense fears that often come with relationships.

Low self-esteem is common among people who did not form secure attachments with their caregivers. Whether you are avoidant and try to stay away from commitment or you are anxious and can't help but worry, it's hard to feel good about yourself when you have an insecure attachment. As a child, neglect or abuse may have made you start to think that you were not good enough for love and care. You might have internalized the messages that caregivers were unconsciously or consciously giving you, or you might have extrapolated information that wasn't entirely accurate because children are not born understanding the complexities of the world. If you have low self-esteem and think that you are unworthy of love or care, that is a sign that you may have attachment issues.

People with an insecure attachment style may struggle to trust other people, and it makes sense that they would be cautious when giving trust to others. When people don't meet your needs, you conclude that you cannot trust other people to provide for you and provide you with love reliably, so you enter the adult world with that same outlook. While you may rationally know that not all people are going to hurt you and reject you, the shadows of your past still look heavily over you, and they urge you to be cautious, and they fill you with doubts. Those doubts can make you anxious in a relationship, and those same doubts can lead to you closing yourself off and becoming avoidant in a relationship.

You may continuously feel unsafe. There may always be a small voice in the back of your head telling you that something is wrong with your relationships and that you need to be ready for when things fall off the rails. You may feel repeating fear that your partner isn't going to give you what you need, and you may think that they are bound to disappoint you at some point despite not having evidence that suggests your thoughts are real. You may feel on edge, and maintaining relationships may be exhausting because you always feel like you need to watch for danger.

You may want to form deeper connections but are too fearful to try, or you don't know how to do so correctly. When you have tumultuous attachments, you may not have a clear idea of how to create the relationships you long to have. In your attempts to alleviate the worries that your partner will leave you, for example, you may engage in self-sabotaging behaviors that prevent you from creating a secure relationship. For instance, you may check your partner's texts worrying that there's something inappropriate in their messages, but doing so can reduce the trust in your relationship rather than creating more trust. Thus, insecure attachment styles can make it hard to have a secure relationship, let alone feel secure in that relationship.

It may also be hard for a person with an insecure attachment style to communicate their feelings or needs. If you have an insecure attachment style, you may not have the emotional tools or awareness to communicate how you are feeling to your partner. You may feel anxious about the relationship but not know how to address that anxiety in a way that helps instead of hurts your relationship. In time, you can learn to overcome those anxious feelings and teach yourself skills that you need to maintain secure relationships that give both you and your partner fulfillment.

How Insecure Attachment Impacts Your Relationships

People with insecure attachments often shroud their relationships with negativity. They expect the worst, and as a result, the bad parts of their relationships tend to get more weight than the good ones. You may also have insistent [1] fears that your partner will not love you enough or will leave you, and that attitude can cause you to accuse your partner of having feelings or completing actions that they didn't have or do. Consequently, misunderstanding often occurs and creates a rift in your relationship.

Anxious attachment can also cause heightened emotions in a relationship, which makes it hard for each partner to express themselves constructively. You and your partner, upon not understanding one another because of ineffective communication, may start yelling at each other. It may temporarily feel good to yell, but in the long run, it doesn't solve your issues, and it doesn't help your partner understand you better.

When you have an anxious attachment, it becomes hard to move forward with your relationship, and you may get stuck in the past or fixate on the future in ways that disallow you to be present in the relationship. When you're worrying, you're not being mindful. You're letting the past control your future, and you're focusing on parts of your life that you have no control over. You cannot decide what happens in the future, just as you cannot change the past; therefore, when you have an anxious attachment, you cannot focus on what is currently happening with your relationship, which makes it hard to deal with the issues that are happening in the moment.

Most importantly, your worries may cause worries in your partner, and all those worries magnify all the other issues in your relationship, and they prevent you from taking steps to make your issues better. While your partner may have a secure attachment style, they still have insecurities and past experiences that will make them hard to see clearly in certain situations. Thus, you can both end up being blinded by your past and fears rather than existing in the moment. The more you let the negative feelings linger, the more they will feed into existing negative ones. They will pull you apart from the relationship you want, even as they try to fool you into believing that they are protecting you from potential harm.

How To Prevent Insecure Anxious Attachment

If you're a caregiver to a young child, you may want to take special attention to ensure that your child does not develop an insecure attachment. While insecure attachment is often associated with abusive or dangerous home environments, that is not always the case. Even seemingly small factors can add up and become much larger. Nevertheless, by being more aware and paying attention to some key behaviors, you can decrease the chances of your child having an insecure attachment.

One of the most important things that you can do for your child is to provide consistency. When you care for a child, you have to ensure that you are responsive to their needs and that you try to be a consistent caring force in their life. While there are sometimes parts of your life that you cannot control, such as injuries or postpartum depression, those issues can cause inconsistency and make it hard for you to care for your child with consistency, you must find a way to ensure that your child has a secure bond with you and that they never feel insecure about your role in their life.

Eye contact with your child is an important method of forming an attachment. For some people with certain conditions, including RAD, it may be difficult to create eye contact. Nevertheless, making the effort to create that connection is a good way to combat any risk factors your child might have for developing an anxious attachment style. Eye contact will also help them in future relationships because it is a common form of expression and bonding when people communicate with one another.

Learn to reflect the way your child is feeling through your words, facial expressions, and gestures. By reflecting their feelings on your own face, you can help them feel acknowledged emotionally, and you will show that you care about their emotional well-being and how they are feeling. Reflecting one another's emotions is an important social quality, so be sure to do it with your child, or else they may miss a crucial level of bonding with you. Showing their feelings reflected to them can show your child how to show empathy and forge connections with other people.

Be sure to give undivided attention to your child. Thus, you should limit how much you are using your phone or other technology during bonding time. You want to make your child feel that they are important to you, and if you are constantly distracted when you care for them, you send the message that they aren't as important to you as other areas of your life, such as work. While you may think that your baby or young child won't notice your distracted state, children pick up on small signals, so it does make a difference.

Be vigilant of the symptoms of RAD, not just in your children but in other children that are close to you as well. Sometimes, conditions beyond your control may cause RAD. By addressing what is in your control, you can usually prevent RAD, but if you are either dealing with a child who had a less ideal caregiving situation before they came to you or who you were previously unable to provide a secure environment, it may be too late to prevent RAD. That child may have already developed the condition and the symptoms, and at that point, all you can do is be aware of that child's mental state and get them the help of a mental health professional if you suspect something is wrong. With increased awareness and early care for this condition, children can learn to form secure attachments before their anxious attachments follow them into adulthood.

2

THE REMARKABLE PATTERNS IN DATING SOMEONE WITH AN ANXIOUS ATTACHMENT STYLE

Why Your Patterns Matter

When you are dating a person with an anxious attachment style, you face unique challenges, and it can be harder to keep the relationship healthy. Only about three percent of women and five percent of men say that they are not committed to their partners; nevertheless, to someone who has an anxious attachment style, they will persistently worry that their partner will not commit to them or will otherwise hurt them due to past experiences. Thus, people who have an anxious attachment style need you to help them create a better perspective of what truly is, and forming healthier patterns is an ideal way to accomplish that goal. Partners must work together to form feelings of security.

Show Your Partner Empathy

Empathy is not just feeling sorry for a person or knowing what their pain must be like; rather, it is an act of taking the time to feel with the other person. Brene Brown says that when you have sympathy, your loved one is metaphorically in a hole, and you are looking down at them from above. However, when you have empathy, you get into the hole with your loved ones, and you sit with them in their pain. Sympathy may provoke you to try to fix a problem your partner is facing or make light of the situation to try to make them feel better, but empathy allows you to listen to them without judgment, and it allows you to see the world from their perspective and emerge from some of the biases you have.

Not only does empathy help your partner to become more vulnerable with you, but it helps you become more vulnerable when you speak to them. When you are empathetic, you open your mind, and you deepen your bond with the other person by paying attention to what they are expressing to you rather than trying to merely wipe away their pain. As a result, you and your partner can be honest, and your anxious partner will have fewer worries about your intentions and your love for them. While empathy cannot fix anxious attachment alone, it eases some of the tension, and it allows you to become vulnerable enough to heal from the hurts that keep you both from having a fully committed relationship.

People, for the most part, are all born with empathy, and fortunately, it is a skill that you can develop. The best way to build empathy is to practice it. You should take time to imagine situations from the points of others. Imagine that you are in their shoes and learn to sit with the negative feelings that other people have rather than trying to neutralize them. As you commit to seeing beyond your small world view, you'll start to improve your relationship, and you'll show your partner that you are willing to give them emotional commitment, and you will go through any hardship with them rather than just as a bystander. Your partner will feel more supported, which alleviates some of their fears.

Appreciate Your Partner

Your partner needs to feel appreciated, or else they will start to fear that you don't love them enough or that they are not doing enough to please you. In return, your partner should show you some appreciation as well. Appreciation motivates people, and it encourages them to do more. Thus, acknowledging the efforts of your partner can promote a stronger relationship and more efficient handling of the life you share. It can be challenging to bring two people's lives together, but if you can appreciate the way you and your partner act as a team, your relationship will become brighter.

Relationship expert, Malini Bhatia of marriage.com, says that many people wrongly have the attitude that they don't need to thank people for small things that they are supposed to do anyway, but this attitude can be a harmful one, she says, because it often indicates that one partner may think that their own contributions are more important than their partner's. Small contributions, such as taking out the trash, cleaning, and cooking dinner, are mundane, but they are vital. If these tasks went undone, you would notice, but because you are so used to them being handled, you may forget how much they matter. Relationships should be balanced, meaning that your contributions should equal out in ways that satisfy you both. If your partner thinks that you do not acknowledge or appreciate their contributions, their insecurities may become very loud. Appreciation often translates as love, and conversely, without appreciation, your partner won't feel loved.

Appreciation can come in many forms. You can appreciate your partner by listening to them without distraction. You can also appreciate them by audibly thanking them for what they do or complimenting their good work. Never be dishonest with your compliments, but you should give them. Mention how their efforts help you do better because that will make them feel like they are a vital part of your life. Further, find beauty in your partner often. Look beyond shallow compliments like "You look hot," and find a compliment that better reflects who they are, such as "That dress shows off your radiance, and you look like you're glowing." Most of all, you need to show your love through your actions, not just your words, to prove to your partner that you are committed to them and care about their well-being.

Be Supportive of Their Interests

Surely, you want to support your partner. If you don't, you are with the wrong person, but the issue of supporting your partner's interests go far beyond just wanting to give them support. Too many people fail to encourage and listen to what their partners like! Hobbies and passions give people motivation, and it helps them fill the time. If you don't have interests, you're going to have a pretty boring life, so you need to embrace your interests and your partner's interests as well. One of the best ways to show you care to an anxious partner is to try to partake in some of their interests and ask them questions about how that interest makes them feel and what they want to do with that passion in the future.

You might not understand your partner's interest, but you need to listen to what they tell you. Give them time and an undistracted ear to express their new project or their progress on a long-term endeavor. Don't dismiss what makes your partner happy just because you cannot relate to those interests. For example, if your partner is interested in the study of bugs, don't say, "Ew bugs, they're just little gross creatures, why would you want to study those?" because that statement expresses judgment, and it can even cause your partner to feel shame, which will reinforce ideas they have about not being worthy!

Never devalue your partner's interests. You may think that the things you like are somehow more cosmically important or influential than your partner's interests, but that attitude will make your partner feel belittled. Thus, you should never let yourself fall into the mindset of thinking your partner's passions are lesser. If you cannot accept the things your partner loves, you are never going to give them the care that they need, especially if they are already anxious. You never have to fake being interested in something you're not at all interested in, but you should be willing to engage in conversation about that thing with the attitude of, "I enjoy this because my partner glows when they talk about this, and I can see how happy it makes them, which makes me happy.

Remind Your Partner of How You Feel

You may feel that your own emotions get lost in the perceptions created by your partner's anxiety. With the following steps, you can learn to remind your partner of how you are feeling so that you don't get stuck in the storm that is anxiety. With these tips, you can get your emotions across without provoking your partner's worries even more.

Talk about your feelings daily. Learning to express how you feel often ensures that problems do not become so big that there's an explosion. When you can be more open with your partner, your partner will sense that you are being open, and they will feel less anxious. If your partner senses that you are hiding feelings, they may start to think that you are hiding other things as well!

Timing matters. Don't start having intense conversations about your feelings when your partner has just gotten home from a stressful day at work, for instance. Make sure that they are in a mental place that is the best fit for a conversation. You must find a time that is good for both of you. Also, be careful not to impulsively jump into a conversation when you are feeling highly emotional because, in those circumstances, a conversation can easily devolve into a shouting match.

Get to the point quickly. Being concise can make sure that you don't inundate your partner with emotions too quickly. Giving them time to process smaller statements can make the process of sharing become more of a dialogue, and it will prevent both of your emotions from becoming too intense.

Start your statements using "I" rather than "you." You make it sound like you are accusing your partner of something while starting a sentence with "I feel…" can cause less friction.

Remember that you cannot change your partner or fix them. No matter how much you may want to get rid of their anxiety, they have to put in the work to improve their issues, and all you can do is be there for them and facilitate a good environment that makes them feel safe as they make changes. You can guide them, but you can never do the work for them. Additionally, remind them that just as you cannot fix how they feel, they cannot fix how you feel either. You need to process your emotions, and trying to get rid of them is only a temporary solution because they won't go away until you learn to process them.

You should avoid becoming aggressive because your aggression will make everyone tenser, and it will always be destructive. Do not step too close to your partner or start shouting. The calmer you can remain, the less attacked they will feel, and the more likely your partner will be to listen and absorb what you are saying. If your partner feels attacked, their brain will respond more defensively, and they will be unable to fully process what you are expressing because of the worry they feel.

Remember that passive aggression doesn't help you. Don't leave a passive-aggressive sticky note to tell your partner how you feel, for example. Instead, express those feelings directly and take steps to clear the air. While passive-aggressive sticky notes are a no, that doesn't mean that you are limited to verbal means of communication. You can write your feelings in a letter, and that still is a direct form of communication. All you have to do is be sure that you aren't avoiding your feelings and that you express them healthily.

There's more to listen to than words. Observe your partner's body language and act accordingly. For example, if you see them crossing their arms, that could be a good indicator that they are starting to close off and that you need to take a new approach. Your partner may not tell you how they are feeling, but their body will give you clues, and you can use those clues to make sure the conversation stays on track and suits the needs of both parties.

Know your partner's anxieties, and keep them in mind when you speak. Try to frame your feelings in ways that they can understand and that appeal to their personality. A big part of communication is knowing how to express what you are feeling in ways that others can relate to and process. If they cannot understand what you are saying, your words will be in vain.

When you express your perspective, be sure to acknowledge that you understand that their perspective may be different. Say something such as, "I am feeling this way, but you seem to be feeling this way." When you use that kind of empathetic language, you can show them that your feelings are not superior, but they are still yours. This attitude will create a better chance of mutual understanding, and both of you will feel validated.

Be Vigilant of Their Needs

Your partner has needs, as do you, and if those needs aren't met, they will start to feel anxious. Thus, being more mindful of your partner's emotional needs can create a caring and safe environment for your partner. Part of building a relationship is getting to know how another person gets emotional fulfillment and what gives them security. If you don't know, start to observe their behaviors. When do they get upset? How do they respond to your needs? What makes them relax? Is there something that always seems to soften their anger or anxiety? The answers to these questions can point you towards what your partner craves to have. The more you listen and pay attention, the more you will discover about your partner's needs.

If you don't know, ask. You won't always know what is going on in your partner's head, and you won't be able to discern their needs. In those cases, you don't need to keep feeling around in the dark. It doesn't hurt to ask what they need. They won't always tell you, but they may even give you indirect clues that can point you in the right direction, or they might say, "I just need a nice dinner and a hug," which tells you how you can help, even if it doesn't tell you what caused the issues. Alternatively, they might start talking about worries they have about your relationship when prompted, which can start a necessary conversation, and you can respond in more helpful ways.

If your partner starts to seem more upset than normal, there is probably a reason, so do some investigation and see if you can figure out why they feel the way they do. Maybe they had a long day at work and need a hug from you to feel better. Maybe they called their critical mother and need affirmation. Maybe they feel like they've failed as a parent and need you to listen to their insecurities. The possibilities are endless, but you need to start not only identifying when your partner is in a bad mood but also learning to recognize what they need in those situations.

Always Keep Your Word

Keeping your word helps your partner feel safer in the relationship because when you stick to your promises, you show them that you aren't going to back out of commitments. When you start breaking promises, even little ones, your partner begins to worry that you will soon begin to break bigger commitments. If you don't know that you can do something, don't promise it. Instead, say, "I will do my best," and then genuinely do your best to stick to those expectations. Breaking promises feels like a betrayal to your partner, and it will further any doubts they have about your care for them.

You Both Need Boundaries

Robert Frost said that "good fences make good neighbors," meaning that knowing where one person's property ends and another one's begins creates important distinctions of what each person expects; mental health experts agree that good boundaries make good relationships. Boundaries are parameters that you put in place to ensure that the people in your life do not act in ways that infringe on your emotional or physical needs. For relationships to be balanced, both people need to have boundaries and abide by each other's boundaries. When a person invades your boundaries, you feel unsafe. If you've ever had someone invade your personal space, for example, you know how it feels for someone to trample your boundaries, and it can feel threatening and cause increased anxiety. Thus, when you don't have clear boundaries, you don't have solid expectations either, or it helps people with anxious attachment, especially to have a firm idea of what kind of behaviors they can rely on in a relationship. Boundaries will make you both feel safer, and they will also resist power imbalances in your relationship.

Enforce the boundaries that you need because that is the only way that you can also support your partner's boundaries. When your partner does something that drains you too much emotionally, or that invades your sense of self, tell them so. Don't make accusations when you tell them, but do explain why that boundary is important to you and reiterate that it needs to remain in place. Your boundaries can change, but you get to decide what those boundaries are because you have a right to autonomy and your own body and mind. Your boundaries will make your partner feel more comfortable in the relationship because they won't have to guess what you need from them or what's "too far" for you.

Listen to the boundaries that your partner needs. Your partner needs to feel like their limits will be respected because if you do not respect those boundaries, they will have more fear, and those lack of clear boundaries could destroy the healthy parts of your relationship and limit your communication.

Encourage Your Partner to Express Their Worries

Keeping worries bottled up is destructive for both people in the relationship. So convey to your partner that their feelings are safe with you, and always recognize their feelings as things that are important to them. As you listen to their feelings, do not become defensive. Becoming defensive is a surefire way to set your partner on edge and to make them think that you are not listening. Remember that their feelings are not fact, and they cannot help how they feel, so you need to respect how they feel, even if you do not feel the same way. Again, be empathetic, and try to understand how your partner must feel.

3

HOW SECURE STYLE DIFFERS FROM ANXIOUS ATTACHMENT

In his attachment theory, Bowlby postulated that when a child had a caregiver who was there for them that they would be less likely to feel anxiety than those who did not have that same certainty of caregiving, and further research has shown how these childhood dynamics influence people in their adulthood in all the relationships that they experience ranging from romantic endeavors to workplace behaviors. The worries established in your childhood often echo the ones you face in adulthood. Thus, the perceptions a person makes as a child will shape the perceptions that they make about how people care for them in adult relationships. Once you can understand your current attachment issues, you can start to find the patterns of how they impact your adult relationships, and you can learn to become more secure in your attachments.

People with an anxious attachment often worry about having their loved ones close to them. When their partner is far away, they may begin to feel anxious that their partner won't come back or is staying away because of a lack of love in the relationship. Just as children do, adults also like to be near the people who give us the most care. When you are far away from your loved ones, you may start to become more anxious and feel unsafe because of childhood conditioning. Beyond just romantic relationships, you may also feel nervous letting your child be too far away from you, even though you logically know they need to learn independence, or you may worry that your best friend secretly doesn't want to hang out with you when you don't see them for a while. Having people nearby is important to you, and you want to be near those safe people because they help alleviate your worries about the terrifying world that seems so filled with doom when you have to face it alone.

As a person with an anxious attachment, you might also desperately search for a "safe-haven." The safe-haven is not a place, but it is often a person or people. When you are with a person and your relationship is going well, you feel like you are in a safe bubble. Thus, going home to a partner should feel comforting, and it should make us feel calm rather than anxious. When we feel unsafe, a person becomes a home base for us, and we want to be near them because their influence makes us feel less threatened. Nevertheless, in insecure relationships, the person who should be a safe haven may invoke more fears rather than easing them. You may never feel like you have the safe haven that you crave, and you may desperately try to facilitate safety and order for your own sanity.

People you are attached to are not only your safe haven, but they are also a "secure base." When you have a secure attachment style, you feel safe to try new things and experiment when you have that feeling of security that comes from secure attachment. You are free to be an individual when you have a secure attachment style with other people in your life, but you may feel more constricted when you have anxious attachments because you do not feel that you can safely explore your world without putting yourself and your relationship in danger. As an adult with a secure attachment, you will more easily try new things, and your partner can help you try new things and improve yourself in ways that you would otherwise be too afraid to do.

Separation distress is the idea that when the attachment figure is gone, you will have anxiety when the person you are attached to is not with you. You may start to doubt their motives and feel like you are missing vital pieces of information that pertain to your relationship. You may feel separation anxiety that makes you feel "clingy" and "needy" in your adult relationships. If you have a young child in your life, you've probably noticed how upset they can become when their parent is there, and that's a normal developmental stage for children, but it is a developmental stage that highly impacts adults too. Anxiously attached people also may feel anxious when the person they are attached to is gone, but they will also feel anxiety when that person comes back because, psychologically, they will not feel secure about their partner's intentions. You may doubt that your partner's commitment is as strong as yours, or you may think that they love other people or things more than they love you. You become dependent on the other person for your self-esteem because people with anxious attachment often attribute the perceived issues in their relationships as reflections of their worth as people.

Even securely attached people can feel anxiety related to relationships, but these people experience that anxiety in very different ways than those with insecure attachment, and they feel calm when they are with the other person rather than feeling worried about the other person's love for them or interest in them. Meanwhile, people with insecure attachments often feel more prominent anxiety and are unable to look at situations holistically. If you look at the most important relationships in your life, you may be able to pinpoint how your attachment style impacts you in these various areas. With that awareness, you can begin to combat your anxious dialogue.

The Anxious Dialogue

When a person has an insecure attachment to their partner, they tend to have an anxious dialogue that repeats in their head, and this dialogue forms through past experiences mixed with fears of the uncertain future. If you have an anxious attachment style, you worry that your parents will not be available to give you the love and care that you want. When you have an anxious dialogue, the fears that you have are not always your partner's fault because in many cases, your anxious dialogue is a result of your deeply ingrained fears. Some past issues make it psychologically hard to create and maintain relationships, especially romantic ones, and your anxious dialogue can then rage loudly in your mind.

Bowlby created his attachment theory to discover how infants attach to their parents, but it has since been used and studied among the adult population as well. Researchers, Hazan and Shaver, discovered that the proportion of infants with each attachment style was the same as the proportion of adults with each attachment style. Thus, attachment styles don't go away when you get older and wiser about how relationships work. Regardless of how much logic you have, your attachment issues can persist. Your attachment style especially impacts your romantic relationships as an adult because romantic relationships often share the insecurities of your parental relationships. Most commonly, insecure attachment presents itself as an anxious attachment, and this anxious attachment comes with common cognitive patterns that shape the way you engage with the world. Moreover, it influences whether you can form a healthy adult relationship and maintain those relationships in the long-term. To fix attachment issues, you must address the anxious dialogue that drives your decision-making.

One worry easily becomes dozens of worries. All the worries they have can lead to misperceptions about the relationship. When you have an anxious dialogue, one small seed of doubt creates disastrous results because you start to pick apart everything you think you know about your relationship. People with anxious attachment are prone to all or nothing thinking, so they will either think, "Everything with this relationship is perfect, and it's going well," or they will think, "This one thing went wrong, so that means that everything will go wrong and the relationship will inevitably fail." Because no relationship is perfect, someone with an anxious attachment style will often endure the latter mentality, which can then cause self-sabotaging behaviors.

Self-sabotage is one of the saddest influences of anxious attachment because it takes something good, and it warps that thing into something stressful. When a relationship goes well, you may start to wonder, "Why is this too good to be true?" You will become terrified that the good feelings you have are going to turn sour eventually because your early relationships taught you that people were not reliable and that they would let you down eventually. Thus, you may start to unconsciously try to provoke your partner or pick fights as a way of controlling the emotional fallout of your relationship. It's psychologically easier to be the destructive force in a relationship than to have to anxiously wait as you wonder when your partner is going to disappoint you.

Then, your partner will respond to your behaviors, and they may do so by ending the relationship or getting angry. In other cases, your partner, feeling emotional distance from you, may do wrong behaviors such as cheating. Your partner's immoral behaviors are never your fault, but your self-sabotaging behaviors often worsen issues that already exist in the relationship, and they reinforce the thought patterns you already have because you'll think, "I was right; they don't want me in their life, and they rejected me," when you were the one initially pushing your partner away and deepening some of the rifts in your relationship.

An anxious dialogue is innately critical, and it cannot mediate its criticisms with the positives, so it blinds you from the full nuance of the truth. Your worries become the driving force in your behavior. This dialogue tries to convince you that the world is an endlessly dangerous place and that you need to be careful or you will get hurt. You learn it from your past, but your own anxieties create it. Further, your anxiety thrives when unhealthy behaviors drive you away from what you want. Thus, instead of deepening your relationship, your anxious dialogue may cause you to destroy that relationship. Thus, your anxious dialogue doesn't only hurt your relationships, but it hurts the outlook you use to see the world as a whole.

Your anxious dialogue can begin with an inconspicuous thought like, "My partner hasn't texted me back." There are many good reasons why your partner may not have texted you back. Maybe they forgot, or maybe they're busy. While a pattern of not responding to you can suggest that there are communication issues, the thought that a missed text automatically means you can't trust your partner or that they somehow do not care for you is a negative and erroneous thought pattern. You have created a connection where none exists, and that connection is not your fault. Rather, it is a product of your brain's propensity for creating patterns, and some of the most powerful patterns are the patterns you learned as a child based on your guardians' responses to your needs because those patterns established your idea of what is the norm for human relationships.

You then begin to have bigger thoughts than just that your partner isn't texting you back. You may begin to notice other things, such as your partner being more distant, which may lead to you thinking your partner is cheating on you regardless of any real evidence that they are being unfaithful. You may begin to confront your partner about the issues you perceive, and your partner may tell you that you are wrong. Your partner's denial only increases the intensity of your worries because you think, 'They are lying to me," and that thought creates distrust in your relationship, and that distrust will seep into all areas of your relationship because you worry that if your partner lies about one thing that they could be lying about anything. You become profoundly suspicious, and your anxious dialogue starts to poke holes in everything in your relationship. You can go from a small worry to fearing that your partner is lying about loving you, for example. The anxious dialogue creates a rumor mill that creates unwarranted doubts about your relationship, and while doubts can be healthy, you cannot accept them without investigation, and anxiety keeps you from investigating the true reasons behind issues.

Anxious attachment style makes it hard for you to deepen relationships because you cannot trust other people. You learn to trust people, and you want a secure relationship, but the anxious dialogue takes up so much of your mental space, and it appeals to your primal survival urges. Even when you can care for your primary needs, you still associate care with survival, so a person with an anxious attachment style will worry so that another person's uncertain behavior doesn't catch them off guard. For the anxious attachment type, it feels safe to insulate themselves from the unpredictability of other people as much as they can, and they will focus too much on the tiny odds of something bad happening, rather than looking at the bigger picture or rationalizing that good things can also happen unpredictably.

Your anxious dialogue doesn't only attack your relationship, but it also attacks your sense of self. You begin to devalue not just the worth or sanctity of your relationship, but you start to devalue yourself. You may think that there is something inherently wrong with you that makes you unlovable. The dialogue starts to include worries such as, "I am not enough, and I will never be enough for my partner," and those worries can debilitate you in all areas of your life. You may start to feel worthless not just in your romantic relationship but also in your career, hobbies, and friendships. The more these fears linger, the more intense they become and the bigger wedge they create in your relationship and life at large.

Your anxious dialogue tears you and your partner apart, and it can make your partner anxious and insecure, especially if they do not have a secure attachment style. Everyone, even people with secure attachment styles, get worried periodically and have insecurities that can fuel rifts in relationships, and when you become combatant or fearful of issues that don't truly exist because of your attachment style, you are sending signals to your partner that they may begin to fixate on. For example, if your partner were to suspect you of cheating and they insist that you are cheating even if you aren't cheating, you would start to worry that they didn't trust you, and that insinuation can make you start to act in anxious ways. Thus, both partners suffer when one or both partners have an anxious attachment because you can almost feel that anxiety in the air, and it creates intense tension between partners.

Why Secure Attachment is Worth the Effort

Secure attachment is one of the best things you can strive for because it remedies the issues caused by insecure attachment. Of course, a secure attachment style will not reduce all anxiety in your relationship, and it cannot instantly solve all the issues you have because all relationships have anxiety and issues even with secure attachment styles. Nevertheless, when you have a secure attachment style, you become more resilient to doubts, and you can investigate them with a more holistic approach, and you can mediate your negative thoughts with positive ones. As a result, a secure attachment allows you to have the kind of relationship that you have probably long yearned to have. While it may seem like it's impossible to change your attachment style and attachment styles tend to remain the same over a person's life, the Journal of Personality and Social Psychology says that people can strive to have a secure attachment style, and there are so many reasons your relationship can benefit from secure attachment.

Research shows that when you have a secure attachment style, your relationships are less tumultuous and they last longer. So, if you're looking for a relationship that lasts several months or many years, an anxious attachment style can make that goal feel impossible. When a romantic relationship is secure, it will reflect a secure relationship of an infant and parent with some nuances that reflect the unique nature of adult relationships, so it will be something that feels unconditional and it will feel stable. In a secure relationship, you don't feel frantic that one obstacle will destroy the relationship. You feel cared for and you feel safe, and in adult relationships, you and your partner are a team who care for each other.

People with secure attachments with their partners can commit to honesty without worrying how your partner will respond to your honesty. Therefore, secure attachments create trusting relationships and communication when things start to go wrong rather than blowups when tensions have been mounting. The doubts of your anxious dialogue can never facilitate trust because they make you skeptical of all the good parts of your relationship. Thus, secure attachment helps you see all the wonderful things a partner can offer.

Your attachment impacts your ability to be intimate, and when you have a secure attachment, you can engage in intimate relationships, while insecure attachment styles may make intimacy hard. When you can create intimacy, you will feel safer with your partner. One study asked questions of seventy couples to evaluate their attachment and how it impacted their intimacy and overall closeness. They also did several activities, such as yoga, to facilitate closeness. The results showed that the activities helped partners feel closer, and they could lessen some of the impacts of insecure attachment. Another study showed that sharing each other's feelings through journaling could also create more security in relationships, and people with insecure attachment most needed this communication to create a connection with their partners. Thus, even small acts can start to create intimacy in your relationships, and these steps are critical for combatting your anxiety.

A secure adult relationship allows partners the space to exist as individuals just as they exist as a pair. When you have a secure relationship, both you and your partner feel safe in that relationship, so you feel free to express your interests as an individual without fear of retribution. Ultimately, secure attachment makes you feel more like yourself when you are in a relationship. You can like things that your partner doesn't like just as your partner can like things that you do not like. When you don't have a secure relationship, you may worry that if you disagree with your partner that they will stop loving you or otherwise reject you. Security allows you to exist without the self-depriving force that is insecurity, so you can maintain your identity as an individual while still being part of a unit with your partner.

When you have a secure attachment, dependence does not take away your ability to feel safe. While it is always good to have some individuality in a relationship, relationships also encourage some degree of dependence. This dependence does not make you weak, but it shows that you are willing to rely on someone else and put your faith in them, which is one of the most rewarding parts of any relationship.

4

YOUR BRAIN AND RELATIONSHIPS

As much as your brain and your heart seem like two completely different forces, your physical and emotional processes are inherently connected, and they work together to maintain your well-being. Research widely shows that when you have poor physical health outcomes, your mental health is worse, just as when you have poor mental health outcomes, your physical health can also decline. For instance, when you have high levels of distress, you are nearly one-third percent more likely to die from cancer. Additionally, when you have conditions like heart disease, diabetes, obesity, or many other physical conditions, you are more likely to develop mental health disorders, and you are more prone to stress. Therefore, the link between your mental health and your physical health is well-established, and your brain processes are highly impactful on your emotional responses and ability to forge relationships.

Understanding the Nervous System

The nervous system is one of the most critical parts of your body because it helps you respond to stimuli, and it contains your nerves and neurons, which create a network that connects the various parts of your body. Your nervous system is how you make sense of the sensations of your world, and this includes signals related to survival, which you rely on your parents to fulfill when you are a child. The nervous system controls all your reactions because the nervous system sends signals that allow you to process stimuli and use thought processes. Accordingly, any responses that you have in a relationship, or any part of your life, are dictated by three processes: stimulation, integration, and output. Your body first has something to set off the nervous system response, your nervous system then utilizes that data and decides what to do with it, and then, as a result, you make decisions. Sometimes, those decisions are unconscious, but other times, they take longer to process and are conscious.

You can divide your nervous system into two parts; your central nervous system (CNS) is the nervous system that connects your brain and spinal cord, while the peripheral nervous system (PNS) connects the other areas of your body. The CNS uses the cues from the PNS to use information that the rest of your body has sensed. Your spine is in charge of reflexive responses that occur, such as muscle twitches, so some of your PNS reactions happen before you fully process what is happening.

Every person's PNS is subdivided into multiple parts: sensory division and motor division. The sensory division is the one that picks up on stimuli, and so it is what will tell you that your hand is on a hot object. The motor division is what will make you take action, so it is what will cause you to pull your hand away from the hot object. You can subdivide the motor division into parts of its own: the somatic response and the autonomic response. The somatic part of your system is responsible for voluntary responses, while the autonomic part is responsible for involuntary response, which includes stomach functions, heartbeats, and breathing. The autonomic part has a sympathetic division, which thrusts the body into action, and the parasympathetic division, which calms the body. Thus, the way your body has trained your nervous system to respond can impact all decisions and actions.

The sympathetic nervous system is responsible for your fight or flight response. This response is an unconscious response that helps your body react in dire situations. In a dire situation, you will either take action, run away, or sometimes, you might even freeze. These actions happen before you can process what you are doing, and if you feel anxiety in a relationship, you may react based on stimuli before you've given yourself the time to process all the information you are receiving. Thus, while your normal responses can save you in some situations, they can also complicate your ability to interact with other people and form healthy relationships.

With all that in mind, your nervous system shapes many of your responses, and it shows that you cannot disconnect your body from how you feel because your experiences form how your nervous system reacts in the future. You don't have to keep having a negative response. You can train your brain to think in more helpful ways. All it takes is becoming more conscious about your behaviors and your feelings, as well as pushing yourself out of your comfort zone just a little.

The Speed of Thoughts

In his book, Thinking, Fast and Slow, Daniel Kahneman excellently details how your body's natural reactions influence how you think. There are various systems in the brain responsible for your reactions, and these systems are composed of multiple complex systems, which are much more complicated than most people can easily understand, so for simplicity's sake, Kahneman tells the readers to imagine that their brain has two systems, System 1 and System 2. System 1 is responsible for what is called "fast thinking." This thinking is the product of your fight or flight response, and it is the thinking that you most often do. It is unconscious and doesn't require much time, so you can come up with a response instantly. It also takes little energy to exert and is as natural as thinking gets. It is how you can intuitively know that one plus one is two. Meanwhile, it probably takes you longer to think of what seventy-five times seventy-two is, and that's where the second thinking comes in, which is the slow thinking.

The second system of your brain is much more exhausting to employ. When you have to slow down and consciously process a situation, you use this part of your brain. The issue with this part of the brain is that it is lazy. System 2 doesn't like to do work when it doesn't have to do any work, so it often defers to the judgments of System 1. Further, system 2 is laborious and languid. If you're in a life or death situation, you don't have time to use this system. For example, if you see a bear approaching you, you probably aren't going to stand there for ten minutes trying to weigh out the pros and cons of each option you have. You'll react instantly based on your instincts because waiting to consciously think the situation through could be deadly.

In modern times, there are fewer life or death situations. Nevertheless, many situations still feel that urgent based on your conscious responses. As a child, for example, if a caregiver does not feed you promptly, those experiences may make you start to feel anxious whenever you get hungry. You may then eat the quickest thing you can find based on System 1 judgments rather than processing what would nutritionally be best for you. Thus, issues in childhood can feel threatening long into adulthood, and attachment issues arise to protect you from potential harm even when you are safe.

The Mind and the Heart

While the mind and the heart are often dichotomized in battles against your brain and your heart, these two forces are more connected than you might think. Your brain deals with all your thoughts and emotions, and it translates those things into action. You may have certain thoughts that you never act on, and it is up to your brain to make judgments based on what you know, what you feel, and what you have experienced. When you have experienced traumas, your brain will go to extra lengths to try to avoid that pain ever happening again, so while humans like to think they are rational creatures, so much of human behavior is emotional and experiential. Thus, to separate your mind from your heart is a grave mistake that will never bring you relationship harmony.

Your amygdala is the part of your brain that focuses on negativity for the sake of survival, and it is the part of your brain that becomes engaged when you have a fight or flight response. It is associated with processing emotions and giving them meaning, and it engages when you have an emotional response. Thus, the amygdala can hold onto past actions and give them more meaning than they deserve, and it can make you unaware of your behaviors because fear blinds you. You act on that fear rather than turning to your system 2 brain and letting it think your actions through. As a result, you may also act in ways that other people acted towards you. Not only do you expect the same treatment that your parents gave you, but you might also give that treatment to other people. You may become worried that your partner may not love you, and in the process, you start to insult and belittle them for behaviors that you think are the problem.

Your past relationships taught you what to expect in current relationships, so it is the past rather than the present that most impacts the dialogue you have running through your head. One study from John Hopkins suggests that people who have more positive outlooks live longer, and that study shows the power of positivity. Often, negative thoughts stick out more to you than positive ones because you're in the pattern of assuming the negative. Five positive comments may pale compared to one negative one, and when you challenge those negative thought-patterns, it helps to notice the positive thought patterns that you can choose instead. The more you reiterate this positive thought pattern, the more it challenges the negative priming that you learned in childhood.

You cannot erase your negative thoughts, but you can rewrite the dialogue in your brain. Your brain likes the path of least resistance. It likes to resort to that habitual System 1 brain, but if you become more self-aware, you can slow down and force yourself to take the harder route. The more you do it, the easier it will become. Within months or years, you can eliminate the negativity because the path of positivity becomes the path of least resistance.

Relationship expert, John Howard, works with many clients, often in high-ranking business positions, and the first thing he asks them is about their relationships with their parents because, as this book has detailed, those relationships are foundational and are one of the best indicators of what problems you may have in current relationships. You may see qualities of your mom or dad in your partner without even realizing that you make these associations unconsciously—the patterns you experienced become the most foundational patterns.

Much of what you do each day is automatic, meaning that you do not consciously think about it. Forty percent of what you do each day is habitual, and so you often rely on past experiences to shape what you will do in the future. Your habits for surviving childhood experiences are habits that you continue into adulthood. Some of those coping mechanisms may be unhealthy. For example, if as a child, you learned that you had to yell for other people to hear you, you may escalate from disagreeing with a partner to having a full-on screaming match because of your anxieties. That approach doesn't get much done, but it helps you feel less powerless at that moment. As a child in a difficult situation, sometimes constructive processes are not beneficial because you don't have the power to assert yourself, so all you can do is get through it, but many situations do benefit from constructive behaviors.

Sometimes, you need to break habits and challenge the way you normally go about your relationships. It may feel uncomfortable, but it takes you away from the normal thought processes that keep you stuck in your anxious attachment. To challenge the relationships of your past, you need to show yourself that relationships can be different. If you do not work through uncomfortable feelings and try to run away from them, you're going to keep repeating the old patterns of your relationship. Habits can take months or even years to break, but no matter what habit you have for dealing with hardship, you can relearn better ways to replace those methods that got you through childhood hardships but didn't help you move forward.

Howard suggests that people think about the way they craved their parents' love and how they tried to get that love. In some cases, there was no way to get that love, but children would still try to be perfect for attaining the care they strived for. Some parents, perhaps from issues stemming from their own upbringings, simply cannot give children the care they crave to have. The standard for love and that fruitless feeling of not being good enough make it hard to feel like unconditional love and care are possible.

Children, on average, are scolded eight times as often as they are encouraged, which is a gross imbalance that shows why so many people are trying and failing to meet impossible standards. They think that they have to reach lofty heights to be loved, and that's not the case, but it's no wonder that those same negative thoughts often are the ones that tear relationships apart. Those thoughts are what create that nasty dialogue in your head, but research shows that positive reinforcement is more impactful in changing one's behavior than negative feedback, and that's because children and adults alike respond to positivity and praise. When we don't get that, our anxieties increase. No parents are perfect, so even people with secure attachments can still have that feeling of being unworthy, but attachment issues only exacerbate that feeling of being unlovable.

When you have attachment issues, your perception of what normal relationships look like will be different. Thus, you need to address those issues if you want to move forward and engage in more positive experiences. As a child, if your dad was an alcoholic, you may start to worry when your partner drinks, or if your mom was unfaithful, you might worry that your partner will be unfaithful too. Your partner may leave for a run in the middle of the day, and maybe that's the same excuse your parent once used when they were drinking or cheating. You will see similar patterns in your partner, and you might come to conclusions that are not realistic, but your conclusions make sense because your intuition created them. They are the part of your brain that is trying to keep you safe from the potential pain that an addicted or unfaithful partner might cause. In another example, for someone with a secure attachment, a disagreement is unpleasant but part of normal relationships. Yet, to a person whose parent was abusive and would hit them during fights, any disagreement can feel threatening based on the pattern that they established in childhood. Thus, a wide range of situations can influence how a person responds in adult relationships, and you have to learn to recognize what patterns rule your reactions.

Because of the amygdala response, many people are afraid of vulnerability because when you are vulnerable, you open yourself up to a potential attack. You give them a chance to hurt you if they are so inclined, which is scary. Nevertheless, vulnerability leads to intimacy, and emotional intimacy is vital in a healthy relationship because it shows your partner the deepest parts of you. Often, the things that you are afraid to show are often the things that other people will love the most about you because they make you unique. The vulnerability lets you love more, but for anxiously attached people, it is hard to hand over that trust.

Plato's allegory of the cave explains the scary mental processes that people have to the uncertain. In this allegory, there is a cave, and people have tied prisoners to chairs, and the prisoners must watch shadows on the wall that a fire and figures placed behind them form. They have never seen anything else. The shadows are what the chained people think that the world is, but then one of the prisoners escape, and they realize that there is a wall behind him and a fire that created the illusion of the creatures on the wall. The escaped person goes back to others and tries to tell them about the fire and figures, but no one believes him because all they see are the shadows. Eventually, the prisoner goes a step forward and steps out of the cave. At first, the light is blinding, but then, as his eyes adjust, the freed prisoner realizes the beauty of the outside world.

Plato created the allegory to show how people's perception of what is commonly wrong, and that knowledge can be scary and that it is often easier to remain a chained prisoner who thinks that what he sees is all that is. Nevertheless, when you do not face the bright light of what is beyond the surface, you miss out on the beauties of the world, and you are stuck in the darkness. The darkness is your anxiety and your inability to allow vulnerability in your relationship, and it will continue to hurt you until you force yourself to step into the light and challenge the status quo.

Ultimately, no one will love you the way you want unless you let them know you, so to have a fully enriched relationship, you need to push past your worries and share new parts of yourself. As a response, your partner will also become more open because when you aren't open with them, they become worried about your commitment to them. While your brain might try to resist your attempts at vulnerability because of past pain, you need to keep in mind that the best relationships always come with emotional risk because no matter how much you try to protect yourself, you cannot prevent bad things from happening just as so many good things won't happen if you don't defy negative thought patterns.

5

STRIVE TOWARDS SECURE ATTACHMENT STYLE

If you want your relationships to improve, you need to begin to work towards a secure attachment style and leave behind your anxious attachment style because if you don't, you will hold yourself back from happiness. This work will not be easy because anxious patterns have become ingrained in you, and it could take months or years to establish patterns that resist those old ones. Nevertheless, you must put that effort in if you want any hope of having the calm, soothing relationships that you probably desire. While the full treatment takes a long time, you will likely start to see change very soon after you begin some new habits

Know What You're Up Against

Before you can do anything else, you must acknowledge your anxious attachment style. Hopefully, you have already figured out what your attachment style is, but you need to do more than just put a name to it. You must admit to yourself that this style is a part of you and acknowledge that it has some degree of power over you. It can be hard to admit that something controls your behavior, but you need to admit that if you want any hope of changing it because while it may control you, awareness will allow you to control it.

Think about the various relationships you have in your life, and contemplate how you react in those relationships. Anxious attachment often looks similar case to case, but you will have a unique set of behaviors that you'll want to discover. It's time to get more than academic and begin to analyze which anxious attachment tendencies you have. Do you tend to worry your partner will cheat on you? Do you worry that your partner will leave you because you are not worthy? Do you check in on your partner often or look at their phone without permission? Do you try desperately to cling onto them? Asking yourself these kinds of questions will show you what you're up against.

Keep a journal that notes your progress. While many people scoff at the idea of journaling, it is actually one of the most impactful behaviors you can choose to do. Journaling helps you better understand your patterns, and it allows you to make connections when it otherwise would have taken you longer to make those same connections. Journaling is scientifically proven to be good for your health. Research shows that journaling for around fifteen minutes per day over several months reduces stress. When you reduce your stress, you can look at situations with a clearer head. Moreover, journaling will also improve your physical health by decreasing your chance of illness, sharpen your memory, and boost your mood. Those are just a few of the bonuses! The main benefit, of course, is that it helps you see how far you have come and how far you have yet to go.

Commit yourself to recovery from your anxious attachment. While change is always scary, you need to embrace that change and decide that you are going to give this process your all. If you only give marginal efforts and don't commit because of doubts you may have, you will never reap the benefits, and you will continue to struggle as you try to balance relationships. When you start to know what it is that you have to face, it will become easier to commit because once you know what you will have to face, you can begin to see the important patterns that will influence how you address the challenges that come into your path.

Reshape Your Thoughts

The thoughts you have that reinforce your anxious feelings will resist treatment. Because the human brain seeks to find patterns and make sense of the world based on your experiences, it can commonly create cognitive distortions, which are thoughts that you believe are true even though your perception is off. For example, if your parents often neglected you, you come to expect that every person will do the same and that they "Don't think you are worth the effort of caring," based on past information that is not universally true. You assume the information you have will always be valid, and in the process, you can self-sabotage relationships that defy your cognitive distortion. In the face of cognitive distortion, you need cognitive restructuring, a process that helps you reorient your thoughts.

Use the ABC method. The ABC method is a model that Dr. Albert Ellis created to help people see the links between their thoughts, emotions, and actions. It is a commonly used method in cognitive-behavioral therapy. Cognitive-behavioral therapy (CBT) is a type of therapy that seeks to address negative thought patterns and rewrite them so that clients can have healthier behaviors and thought-processes. The ABC model is an acronym for activating event, beliefs regarding the event, and the consequences of the event. It is the B that bridges the gaps between A and C, and it is the primary focus of CBT. The activating event is what sets off the thought-process, and it can be something like your partner not saying hello to you in the morning. This activating event then can cause negative thought patterns, which can then cause negative emotions, such as feeling hurt, angry, or sad. The negative thoughts you have are the beliefs, and the emotions or actions that correspond are the consequences, so in the partner scenario, you may start to think, "My partner doesn't love me," based on just that one incident, and then those anxious thoughts may result in you feeling devastated and acting out. When you use the ABC method, you try to break down your thought processes, and you can learn to challenge the beliefs you have, which insecurities deepen if you let them.

Avoid common thought tendencies. People who experience anxious attachment and other mental issues all fall back on similar thought-processes, which can do more harm than good, and you need to learn these patterns and stop them from recurring. Challenge your all or nothing thinking. The world has gradients in it, so while a mess-up may seem like the end of the world, it probably isn't. Not every situation has a clear right or wrong, and that's okay. You don't need to get into the mindset that you are either winning or losing, wrong or right, good or bad. People can be many things at once, and when you realize that, you become less critical of yourself and others. Further, don't expect the worst. Just because something bad can happen, it doesn't mean that it will. It's easy to jump to the worst conclusion, so slow down and think about what's really happened. Also, be careful of overgeneralizations because overgeneralizations can make you believe that certain things are universally true when that is not the case. Your partner saying that they don't like something you made for dinner, for example, is not an attack on your skills as a cook. One cooking mishap doesn't mean you *always* cook terribly, and your partner may genuinely just not like the flavors because of their personal tastes. Thus, you need to be aware of these tendencies to think in extremes so that you can mediate your thoughts.

Monitor your thought patterns. If you want to effectively challenge your thought patterns, you have to act like a security guard and catch them as they sneak into your head. Once you get rid of certain negative-thought patterns, that doesn't mean you are safe. Negative thought patterns are going to want to continue to form in your brain, but you need to catch them before single thoughts become habitual ones. Learn to spot when you are overgeneralizing or oversimplifying situations and remind yourself of how what you are tending to think is false.

Challenge what you assume to be true. A big part of this process is questioning everything. Doubt can be a destructive force, but scholars suggest that doubt is necessary to have faith because if you blindly believe in something, that belief is fragile. Yet, if you challenge that belief and scrutinize it, you either debunk it, or that belief becomes stronger. To have faith in your relationship, not just a fragile faith, you need to challenge your assumptions and either prove them false or true. With that in mind, you shouldn't be crossing boundaries or creating distrust in your relationship to accomplish this task. Rather, you need to look inward at how you are thinking rather than what your partner is doing.

Address Your Shame

Shame is one of the most destructive forces in any person's life. While guilt is a feeling based on actions that we have done and held ourselves accountable for, shame is a feeling that stems from our negative perception of ourselves. People feel shame when they feel they have infringed on norms or standards that society at large holds them to. Shame can be dangerous, and research has suggested that people with high levels of shame tend to have lower self-esteem. Additionally, researchers Tangney and Dearing found that shame makes people more prone to psychological illnesses, such as depression and substance abuse. Women are especially prone to shame, but men and gender-nonconforming people experience it as well. Most people feel shame at some point in their lives, but when that shame becomes chronic, it reinforces the feelings that fuel your anxiety. Thus, until you address your shame, it becomes hard to move forward and become securely attached.

Determine what makes you feel shame because those are probably the things that also make you feel anxious in relationships. Differentiate shame from things you need to do better because they are not the same. While there may be some overlap between the two, the things you feel shame about speak to how you feel as a person, while the things you need to improve speak to what you want to be as a person. Shame doesn't have to be warranted. Many people feel shame about things they can't change just because those things don't match what other people expect. Thus, while the things that make you feel shame may seem like things you need to change because of outside pressures, you may just need to shift your mindset. When you shift your mindset, you'll start to focus on doing better rather than feeling worse.

The next thing you need to do is stop hiding your shame. When you hide your shame, you make it more shameful. Shame thrives in secrecy. It makes sense why you wouldn't talk about your shame because that shame makes you feel like there's something wrong with you. No one wants other people to look at them in that same way, so they keep their shame to themselves. The shame grows, and it becomes a festering secret that can cause a rift in relationships. When you are vulnerable and open up about your shame, the potency disappears because you no longer have to worry about how other people would respond to you if they found out. After all, when you keep something to yourself, you become more anxious about how people might react if they knew.

Address your shame and reframe it. While you may think you deserve the shame you feel, it's important to confront that shame and determine what you're really feeling. Even when you have actually done something wrong, shame places the attention on you as a person, while guilt focuses on your actions and the impact of those actions on other people. Thus, often when you feel shame, it is more helpful to realize that you are feeling guilt. While shame will tell you that you are a bad person, guilt chances that dialogue and insists that your actions were bad. When you see yourself as inherently wrong, you feel unable to change your behaviors, but when you start to see that bad behaviors don't automatically make you a bad person, you can address your behaviors and ensure that you do better behaviors going forward.

One moment never defines you as an entire person. If you suggest a flawed idea in a work meeting, that doesn't mean that you are always wrong. If your partner doesn't want to do a certain activity with you, that doesn't mean that they think you're weird. People are complex, so you cannot reduce others or yourself to just a few moments. Your shame will convince you that you are inherently flawed, but if you learn to look more holistically and break from the shame, you will start to see that you are so much more than you give yourself credit for.

Create a Foundation of Self-Esteem

When you have self-esteem, it is easier to address the anxious thoughts that influence your attachment style. This book will discuss more on self-esteem later, but you need to begin by creating a foundation for that self-esteem and then allowing it to blossom as you become more comfortable with yourself and your needs. This foundation will not automatically give you heaps of self-confidence, but it will ease you into the process and set you in the right direction.

Find things to love about yourself. Each day, you should look in the mirror and tell yourself five things that you like about yourself. If you can't name five yet, start with just one and build up from there. Look beyond just your physical appearance and think about your personality and behaviors. What have you done well? How do you make the world a better place? What's your role in the lives of other people? Everyone has good qualities, just as everyone has bad qualities, and when you take time to emphasize the good, you feel better about yourself, and you don't as quickly assume that you're not worth other people's attention or love.

Discover what makes you happy. Your hobbies and recreational activities should be things that you genuinely enjoy. Start thinking about what makes you really happy. This task seems simple, but so many people lose track of themselves in the interests of other people. This tendency is especially common among people with low self-esteem because people with low self-esteem often try to change themselves because they want to fit in and be loved. Ironically, that camouflaging of their true selves means that no one can truly get to know them. They can never create the feelings they want because no one ever knows who they really are. They are hiding their true selves, and they are ashamed. You shouldn't feel like you need to go for drinks with a date if you don't like drinking, for instance! Your date may love it, but if you aren't having a good time, they will notice and think you are uninterested in them. Learn to acknowledge your true interests, even if they aren't popular ones.

Be more mindful about your use of technology. While your phone, computer, and other devices are no doubt a great blessing, they can also influence your self-esteem heavily, which will deepen your attachment problems. In a study of young people, the Royal Society for Public Health discovered that Instagram is the worst platform for self-esteem, likely because of comparison as well as bullying and shaming that can occur on social media. Further, the study showed that when people were on social media for longer than two hours that they were more likely to have distress and mental illness. You don't need to cut your social media and technology use, but it will make you feel better about yourself when you are more mindful of its role in your life.

Be prepared to look at the world in new ways because as you start to build a foundation of self-esteem, you will look at yourself and others in so many profound and new ways.

Be Merciful With Yourself

If you are not merciful with yourself, it becomes hard to accomplish goals, and you will always feel that you are missing the mark. So, you need to learn to be kinder to yourself. Positive self-talk is one of the best ways to transform negative thought processes. When you use positive language, you emphasize your good qualities. Additionally, you should learn to admit when you make a mistake, but you should also know that mistakes are not failures, but they are chances for growth. While mistakes are never fun, you can use them to make better decisions in the future and become a better version of yourself. You surely put a lot of pressure on yourself, and you probably put the pressure of expectations on relationships, so be patient and know that mishaps are part of the journey. Your inner critic will dispute mercy, but you should become critical of your inner-critic and remind yourself that no person is perfect. You don't expect your best friend to be perfect, so you shouldn't expect it of yourself either. Being forgiving of yourself is sometimes the hardest thing that you will ever do, but it is necessary for your peace of mind.

Seek Help

Some people will need additional support to help them challenge their anxious thoughts and reach secure attachment. There are several ways that you can tell that you may need some additional help. When you feel like you cannot resist your issues alone, that's a good sign that you need help. You may also have complex issues that you cannot understand without further analysis. Additionally, you may want help with identifying and addressing your limiting beliefs. Whatever the reason for needing more help, do not feel shame that you cannot handle treatment on your own. Look for a mental health professional that specializes in areas that you struggle with, and be persistent about treatment. You might not find the right provider at first, so experiment until you find someone you mesh with and who seems to understand your issues. Mental health treatment may seem like a waste of time or energy, but it is an investment in your future, and it can help you work through your issues more speedily and safely.

6

THE ULTIMATE DATING EXERCISES

The Dating Dilemma

It is hard to date when you have an anxious attachment style, and you may feel like you'll never get the relationship you want. First dates may start well and then quickly spiral as old anxieties already begin to creep up. You might find yourself worrying about whether you will get a second date and, in the process, neglect to be attentive on your date. You may be scared even to start dating when you're anxious about what might happen. Thus, many people stop being present on dates when they have an anxious attachment style because they can't let go of all the worries that something might go wrong. Further, if you get past the first date and establish relationships, your relationships may end prematurely if you don't get a hold of the roots of your issues. While dating can be a major dilemma for anxious people, it doesn't have to be. When you apply some of the following exercises, you can learn to transform the way you date forever.

Daily Exercises

There are daily tasks you can employ to improve your anxiety when you date. These tasks can help you if you are casually dating, or they can help you if you want to be or are in a more serious relationship. Whatever the stage you are in, learning to be more open with yourself and your feelings can help you learn to defy your anxiety and become closer to people. All humans need closeness to thrive, so when you go without it, you are only hurting yourself, and you deny yourself so many of the joys that come with being alive.

Take time for physical intimacy. You don't need to be sexual, though that is certainly a choice you can make, but each day, you should strive for cuddling, hugging, kissing, or whatever other tactile activity that makes you feel closer to your partner. If you do not have a partner at the moment, you can take time to hug friends or other loved ones and have some kind of physical closeness to them. When you can create that physical attachment, your anxiety will start to ease, and you'll get into the habit of being more open with your body and allowing other people to get physically close. Once you let people get physically close, they can then also get emotionally close as well.

Learn to let your partner or date talk for ten minutes without interrupting them and have them do the same for you. While communication shouldn't work like this all the time, you can practice this exercise once each day to ensure that each person learns to listen better. By giving each person a dedicated time to talk, no one feels like other people are talking over them, and you learn to wait to respond until you've heard fully what your partner has to say. When you don't listen fully, you can jump to conclusions and react based on anxiety before understanding the complexity of the situation. Everyone deserves a chance to speak their mind, and when someone doesn't get that, they will start to feel insecure, and you can blow minor issues out of proportion.

Have a daily chat about what each person needs and how they felt the other didn't meet their needs. When you're in a relationship, you need to express your needs each day. It doesn't have to be a long chat— five minutes or so will do— but you should feel comfortable enough to address any issues before they grow out of control. If you're in a more casual or young relationship, you don't have to do this daily, but you should communicate your feelings and concerns whenever your issues arise. You should also strive to have those open dialogues in other relationships, and doing so can be great practice. Unfortunately, not everyone responds well to these kinds of talks, but you must try to facilitate them to have strong relationships that don't become passive-aggressive or clingy.

Take time to indulge one another's interests. A partnership means that you are a team with another person, and it doesn't matter if they like things that you don't understand, you still need to appreciate the other person's interests. If you dismiss what they like, they will start to feel shame, which provokes anxiety. Expect that your partner respects your interests just as you respect theirs. Try to participate in that interest to some degree; at the very least, inquire about that interest and let them express how they feel about it. It is important to show interest in what your partner loves to do, but you should also find special interests that you both can share. Find things that you both enjoy and that allow you to do more together. If you don't have activities to share, you will feel disconnected, which adds to your anxious feelings. Both people's passions are part of their relationships, so don't let those passions become detached.

Make relationship goals. You should both make goals about what you want out of the relationship, and you can check-in on how those goals are progressing each day. These goals are valuable because they help you clarify what you both need and want. As a result, no one feels like they are left behind in the relationship or that they have to sacrifice too much because goals ensure you take the journey together!

Mindfulness Exercises

Mindfulness is one of the most important qualities you can have in a relationship because it allows you to be in the moment without the past pulling you back or worries about what might happen can distract you from what is currently happening. Observe how you feel when you are with new or established partners as you are with them. Use your various senses to ground you in the moment. What does the room look like? What expression is on the other person's face? How do you feel? What taste is on your tongue? When you become in touch with your senses, you stay present. This mindfulness should continue after dates as well. Take time for reflection after dates. Think about how you feel after the date. Did you have fun? What made you uncomfortable or unhappy? What future do you see for that relationship? Sometimes, dates don't go well, so take any rejection in stride and don't let it overwhelmingly influence future dates. Remind yourself that you have a present to make better rather than being pulled into your past relationship woes. When you are mindful with your dating, you allow room for growth, reflection, and you avoid letting past encounters drag you backward.

Vulnerability Exercises

Vulnerability is hard for people with anxious attachment styles. Vulnerability is the ability to be truthful about how we feel, what scares us, and what we want and need. This vulnerability ultimately allows us to connect with other people. Renowned psychological researcher, Brene Brown, discovered how imperative vulnerability is for relationships. She says that people currently tend to be deficient in intimacy, and that deficiency is because people struggle to open up to other people in their lives. Yet, it is hard to maintain a romantic relationship without that intimacy. You need to be vulnerable to facilitate trust, communication, and growth in any relationship.

When you need something, ask for it. Your partner or date is not required to give you what you want, and you shouldn't push them to give you something they are unwilling, unable, or unready to give. If you think your partner isn't being vulnerable with you, share something of yourself first to prompt an open dialogue, but if that doesn't work, you can express that you'd like to get to know them better. If someone does something that is triggering for you, you can tell them that you need them to be more careful with how they speak of that issue. Again, you cannot force them to change, but in a relationship, people should be empathetic and understand the emotional and physical needs of the other person. The issue is that many people don't ask for what they need, so the other person doesn't know that need exists. If you need a hug, ask for a hug. If you need to vent, ask to vent. The answer cannot be yes unless you ask!

Practice expressing your feelings, even if they are not what you think the other person wants to hear. Vulnerability takes time, but you can push it forward by expressing yourself with honesty. If your partner asks you if you are upset, don't say that you are fine just to keep the peace. You are not keeping the peace; you are only shaking the soda bottle so that it will explode when you finally do open it. While opening an unshaken soda bottle will release a little hiss when you crack the cap open, it's only going to cause a mild hiccup. Expressing your upset right away is the best option because if you don't do so, the negative thought patterns have time to sink in, and you can begin to ruminate, which makes you more anxious. It may not be fun to express negative thoughts, but it helps you deal with issues calmly.

When you feel the need to lie to your partner or avoid talking to them about it, ask yourself why you feel that way. There has to be a deeper reason why you are lying to your partner or leaving out information because if there wasn't, you wouldn't feel the need to keep that information secret. Often, you keep to yourself the things that make you feel shame, but remember that shame is a misplaced feeling, and it forgets the complexity of humanity. When you can tell your partner about the thing that makes you feel the worst about yourself, you are showing them the deepest parts of you. Plus, when you share those parts of yourself, you begin to think, "They will love me no matter what just because I am me, and they can love my flaws, even when I struggle to love them." Admitting you're wrong feels dreadful, but it does help people connect.

When you are vulnerable, you can remain true to yourself. You don't just cower in the face of troubles. You deal with the issues head-on, and you let your partner see every part of yourself, especially the ones that are difficult. You show your feelings, and you stop letting shame and fear rule your relationships. Like it or not, you can't avoid sharing difficulty if you want to have any vulnerability. Thus, in whatever ways you can, you need to open the darkest parts of yourself, and as you open those parts of yourself, you let in the light— the hope, the connectedness, and the love.

Trust-Building Exercises

Trust-building is especially important when one or both partners in a relationship have anxious attachment styles because the anxiety can make a person fearful of potential abandonment and that their partner will cheat on them or do other things to break the trust in the partnership. These exercises are both helpful for the person with the anxious attachment and their partner because you must build trust on both sides.

Maintain healthy boundaries. Give your partner the space they need, even when it may tempt you to check on what they're doing. Challenge yourself to lessen how often you check in on your partner. Give your partner the chance to show that you can trust them.

Share information with your partner that they do not know about you, and have your partner share information about themselves that you do not know. No matter how well you know a person, there is always more to learn, so take time to check-in with one another and to deepen the connection you have.

Trust exercises can help you and your partner learn to trust one another more. While this task may feel silly, putting a blindfold on your partner and guiding them through an obstacle course or practicing trust falls can reestablish a missing trust connection between you and your partner. Further, you may want to try other challenges, such as couples yoga.

Communication Exercises

Communication is one of the most vital parts of any relationship because, without communication, you don't have any of the tools that you need to promote vulnerability and trust. Communication allows you to respond to your worries in new ways, and it assures that you talk things through before you react negatively. No matter what your attachment type, but especially an insecure type, you will benefit from these exercises, and all partners should try to complete these tasks regularly for the best results. It's not only time to start talking, but it is time to start communicating in all kinds of ways.

Tell your partner whenever you are feeling anxious, and welcome them to share when they are feeling anxious as well. Again, just as you did when you became more vulnerable, you need to establish an open line of communication for when anyone is anxious and worried about the health of the relationship. You don't have to just limit yourself to speaking.

You can also express yourself using writing, for instance. You can write in a shared journal how you are feeling, and doing so can help you create a conversation without the confrontational elements. With writing, you must be careful not to be passive-aggressive. Don't beat around the bush; be clear about your feelings and problems in your writing.

Communication is so much more than speaking or writing. It is also learning to understand others and reflecting their ideas to them. You must, therefore, learn to listen, and you cannot just listen on the most basic level. Practice active listening. Active listening means that you aren't distracted as you listen, and you give your full attention to other people as they are speaking. You don't try to interrupt them or tell them how they should feel or correct what they are saying. Instead, you take the time to let them tell you how they are feeling and how they perceive the world. When they have said their piece, you can prompt them with questions, again not to tell them how you feel but to try to understand and create empathy. State how you think they are feeling by saying, "I think what you're trying to say here is…" and be upfront about what you don't understand by saying something like, "I'm not clear about that part of what you were saying. Can you say it in a new way?" Eventually, you will get your turn to talk once you have understood as well as you can the other person's perspective, but as you listen, don't try to plan what you are going to say. Fully understand the other person's point of view before you shape your response and express how you are feeling. This kind of mutual listening will assuage any doubts because it will make both partners feel heard.

You and your partner should make greater efforts to show gratitude to one another. Find something to be grateful for about your partner each day. If you are casually dating people, find something about that experience to appreciate. Maybe a date doesn't work out, but you can still be grateful for what that experience taught you or how it will lead you to eventual dates that do work out. Gratitude should be communicative because when you appreciate someone, you should tell them that you appreciate them! While people always assume that dates know they like certain qualities or behaviors, other people cannot read your mind, and they might not even be able to read your body language well. Verbal affirmations make people feel better than being left to assume, so while it might feel corny, everyone likes to be appreciated. Don't give appreciation just for the sake of it, but do give it. Your partner should then give you appreciation in return because you deserve mutual gratitude.

Attempt to spend time each week communicating without the interruption of a phone. You don't need to have your phone out all the time, and you don't need to check your work email when you are on a date. The other person senses the disconnect, even if it is just a brief moment. People want to feel engaged with their romantic interests. You wouldn't like someone else to constantly check their phone. That disconnect would promote anxiety while limiting vulnerable communication because no one wants to be vulnerable when they feel the other person is only half-listening.

When you begin to communicate, you and your partner will have less to worry about. You will become a better date, and you will learn to have deeper, more vulnerable relationships that will leave you feeling self-assured rather than filled with shame.

7

REFORMING YOUR ATTACHMENT STYLE

When you have an anxious attachment style, you've read about and have probably experienced how far-reaching that attachment style is in your life. Experts say that while certain people are prone to certain relationship attachments based on childhood experiences, they also suggest that your attachment style is more fluid than researchers initially expected. Attachment can also shift throughout relationships and based on you and your partner's personalities. Thus, while many variables can reinforce some of your insecure attachment behaviors, you can also use these variables to ease your insecurity in relationships and strengthen your bonds with the people you love.

Know Your Signposts

You have to know what signposts mark your relationship anxiety and learn to redirect yourself in healthier ways. Research shows that people who don't have secure attachment styles often struggle to balance their emotions. When you cannot regulate your emotions, you then have intimacy issues because you struggle to open yourself up to other people. When you start to focus on your behaviors, you can stop yourself when you feel your blood growing hot with insecurity. The insecurity you feel in relationships never comes from nowhere, so learn the signs so that your feelings cannot get the best of you.

Think about the trauma that has shaped you and how it still influences your life. Trauma is the scar you carry after difficult events and that you use to try to keep yourself safe from further damage. The chances are that your insecure attachment style stems from a trauma that you experienced when you were young. While you may say, "My childhood wasn't bad, so I don't have trauma," many people have trauma that goes unacknowledged. Despite having an overall happy childhood, even small events that made you feel unsafe or unloved can have lasting impacts. Frequent criticism from your parents, for example, can leave you feeling unworthy, even when those criticisms stemmed from your parents wanting to keep you safe.

Learn to sense when the anxiety first starts. Each person's anxiety tends to follow similar patterns each time they have it.

For example, it may start as a dull twisting in your stomach and then progress into shaking hands, sweating armpits, and anger. Accordingly, it helps to track how you respond to anxiety in your relationship. Writing in a journal can help you better understand how your anxiety operates. As you write all the details you can down, you'll get a better idea of your triggers, and you'll start to pick up on cues that you didn't notice before. Not every situation will follow the same pattern, but your usual patterns can help you combat most situations that cause trouble.

When you learn to identify when insecurity starts, you can destroy it before it becomes too strong. You begin to take charge of your anxiety rather than letting it take charge of you. Defying your anxiety can be scary, but when you start to creep closer to it, you'll begin to realize that it seems a lot bigger than it really is. Knowing yourself allows you to predict your reactions and practice reacting in new ways. It's hard to break bad habits, especially reactions you've had for years, but if you repeat new behaviors, eventually, the old ones will fade, and they won't be your go-to behaviors anymore.

Consider Your Amygdala

Your amygdala is a part of your brain that handles emotional memories. Thus, when you are having to form a secure attachment because of your old wounds, understanding your amygdala can help you put yourself back on track when you start to feel lost. The amygdala is not good at thinking in gradient. Instead, it either senses that you are in danger or you aren't in danger. There's no, "I might be in danger, but I'm not likely to get hurt." The amygdala reacts as quickly as it can because speed can be the matter between life and death, and it will use your past responses and experiences to shape how you currently respond. When you feel panic or think something is threatening you, try to become conscious of why you feel that way. Think about your childhood and how that influences how you automatically react now. When you are aware, you can start to challenge the assumptions your amygdala makes, and you can rewire your mental processes by making conscious efforts to undermine the thought-processes that harm your relationship security.

Your Feelings Are Important, But They Are Skewed

Feelings are never something that you should take lightly, but they are not a clear view of reality. You need to learn that while what you feel can seem so real, taking a step back can show you that the truth is often so much more nuanced than your initial reactions. Your perspective is always going to be limited, so what you think of your partner may not incorporate what they think of you. You may assume that your partner feels a certain way because of your past experiences, but until you inquire about those feelings, you can never assume that you know how your partner is interpreting a situation. People don't always react in the ways that you expect, so when someone seems outwardly angry at you, they may be hurt or disappointed or angry about things that have nothing to do with you. It's easy to start to worry when you sense something's off with your partner. Listen to your feelings, but do not act on those feelings until you have done a little investigation and have figured out a fuller picture.

Contemplate Your Personality

Your personality and tendencies shape the way your insecurity in a relationship plays out; for example, if you are passive, you may be passive-aggressive, or if you are confrontational, you may yell when you get worried. Whatever your personality is, there are parts of it that will come out and make a sour impression when you start to get anxious. Anxiety about a relationship makes you moodier, and it makes it harder to control your impulses, so you may act on your instincts rather than reminding yourself to stop and handle the situation with a clearer head. When you understand your personality, you can not only reduce the number of destructive behaviors you act on, but you can also learn to use your better personality traits to create communication and relationship growth.

Your personality traits and skills are inherent parts of yourself, so you cannot change them, but you can learn to bring out the best parts of them. When you want to lash out, try to use parts of your personality that create more communication. For example, if you are a natural storyteller who is good at writing, you may communicate best by writing rather than speech. In that case, you can write your partner a letter that expresses your concerns or worries. In another example, if you are organized, you can use that trait to pause and organize your thoughts before you react on impulse, or you can organize a meeting between you and your partner to sort out some of the issues that are bothering you. There are so many creative ways that you can utilize to improve communication in your relationship and promote a more secure attachment style.

Think of Your Partner's Tendencies

Your partner has an attachment style of their own, and they will tend to deal with certain issues in certain ways. Start observing how your partner reacts to their fears and try to brainstorm how you can be more patient when those fears come up. Rather than being defensive, you should try to remind yourself that your partner also has insecurities and that being supportive is the best way to get them to open up. No human is going to be perfect at communicating their needs and understanding their partner's needs, so you need to help fill in the blanks by being more open to your partner's tendencies and learning to work with them instead of changing them. You cannot change integral parts of your partner, but you can help them use those parts in healthier ways!

Learn to Heal Your Inner Child

A hurt child resides in all of us. That child has wounds on their heart, and they expect that they will only get more wounds, so they try to protect themselves from danger, but in the process, they lose track of the light. They get trapped in the darkness, and they want to come out, but they cower in the dark because they are too afraid of the dangers in the light. You cannot forget the child within you that someone hurt at no fault of the child. Think of yourself when you were young, and teach that child that what they want can become true. Show them that they don't have to be afraid. Give them the mercy and the encouragement to heal from those hurts and learn to grow up to be happier and more self-assured.

Visualize Secure Attachment

When you learn to visualize, you increase your odds of desired outcomes in the future. Research suggests that as much as ninety percent of the data that your brain receives is visual. Additionally, your brain can process visual information so much faster than it does other stimuli. According to the University of Minnesota, it can sort through visual information 60,000 times more quickly than text information, for example! Thus, when you can imagine yourself seeing what you want happening, your brain is more receptive to that information, and you can feed your subconscious with your hopes rather than letting negativity form your unconscious behaviors and thought patterns. When you create visuals in your mind, you create a mindset that allows you to have a more secure attachment style.

Imagine yourself in a relationship that doesn't fill you with worry. When you have your insecure attachment style, it is like something is pushing you underwater even though you want to be above the surface, breathing easily. You struggle, but the weight of your anxieties keeps you from the fresh air. Now, imagine yourself bursting through the water. You can swim, you can laugh, and you can engage with your partner without worrying about the day that you'll be back underwater. Your life is lighter, and your relationship doesn't feel like a struggle for your life. By imagining the future freedom you can have in such visual ways, you can remind yourself of what you want and how you'll feel when you get there.

Let yourself be hopeful for the future because there are so many promising relationships waiting for you. The doubt that lingers inside of you only creates a bad image of the future, but you can erase that image and visualize one that you'd like to have. Think about what you want to see in a relationship and how you want your partner to treat you, and as you continue to develop that relationship, use what you have imagined to check in with how you and your partner are doing. Tweak your visualization as needed to reflect your wants as you change and your needs shift. What is good for you now won't be good in the future, so take events as they come and feel free to daydream about a better future.

Remember the Good Instead of the Bad

Remember the good about your partner because it is that good that reminds you of why that person is worth the effort. It's easy to create a long list of all the things that annoy you about your partner and how they must not love you as much as you love them. Instead of finishing that negative list, try to make a list of all the great ways your partner impacts you. When do they make you feel better about yourself? In what ways do they support your individuality? How do they contribute to hobbies you enjoy but that are mostly foreign to them? What about them brings a smile to your face? When you answer these questions, you can see the ways your partner loves you, and with all that in mind, you'll feel better about their intentions the more you rewrite the negative dialogue with yourself.

You should also remember the good about yourself. Don't keep thinking thoughts such as, "I am always the problem. No one will ever care for me because I can never do anything right." Those kinds of thoughts aren't productive, and they make you want to lash out when any little concern appears. Spend some time each day remembering what makes you a good partner. How do you show love to your partner? In what ways do you help them be the better version of themselves? What acts do you hope that they appreciate most? What small acts of love do you do each day? What would you like to tell them most that you have kept to yourself? These questions promote self-awareness and allow you to see your contributions to the relationship.

Know that you and your partner both have constructive and destructive parts of yourself. These parts can cause disaster, but many people use them to promote stronger relationships. You can use your strengths to lessen the impact of your partner's weaknesses, and your partner can strengthen your weaknesses as well. The joy of teamwork is not that you lose what makes you individually great, but it is that you also gain what makes the other person individually great! If you're looking for a secure attachment style, you need to embrace your strengths and weaknesses as well as your partner's.

Know That Each Relationship is Different

Every relationship will have unique challenges and obstacles, so avoid comparing your relationships too much. Secure attachment will look different in each relationship. What promotes security in one pair of partners may change when you swap one of those initial partners out for a new one. These factors can change based on your personality and who has what attachment style! Use the lessons you have learned from past relationships, but don't forget to be flexible because each relationship will have individual challenges. Looking at each relationship as the same reinforces the insecure attachment because it is the notion that, "Well, that's what happened before, so that *must* be what's happening now," that makes it impossible to see the situation in its entirety. You end up making assumptions, and those assumptions can cause you to act in ways that worsen rather than improve the relationship.

Never Sacrifice Yourself

Stick to your values. Your values are a core part of yourself, and they are unlikely to change. For many people, their values give them a sense of purpose, so if you try to change those values for the sake of appeasing the other person, you are sacrificing yourself. If someone cannot accept your values, they never will, and you will always feel trapped in an insecure relationship. While it would be nice to say that every relationship can work if you try hard enough, that's simply not the case. Some relationships will never make you secure, either because you disagree with your partner on core values or your partner is unwilling to accept your needs and try to help you meet them. As a result, you need to decide if a relationship means sacrificing yourself, and if the answer is yes, try to take steps to rectify the situation, which will often work. If a rectification has not worked, you may need to end the relationship.

Don't let yourself get lost in the other person. By having defined boundaries and remaining true to yourself, you can avoid letting your identity be overly defined by the other person's. You need to know where you end, and the other person begins. There will be a lot of overlap in your lives, but you still need to know what limits you don't want to cross. For example, many couples share bank accounts when they have been together for a long time and share the same household, but if you're not comfortable with doing that, you can set a boundary, and that boundary doesn't mean you don't trust the other person, but it marks the degree of autonomy you need to feel safe. You can work up to having a bank account by addressing your insecure attachment, but you can work up to it at your own pace (or not at all). When your partner respects your boundaries, you will trust them more, and you will have less to worry about in the relationship.

Never hurt yourself in the name of hurting someone else. Passive aggression can seem easier than confrontation, but it hurts your relationship and fosters more insecurity because it avoids the true issues. Many people who are passive-aggressive turn to behaviors that hurt themselves more than anyone else. When you are passive-aggressive, it may feel temporarily satisfying, but it doesn't resolve the worries you have. All those worries are still there, compacted down and ignored until something else happens to bring them all up again. The more you ignore those worries, the more you compact them, so whenever they emerge, they do so stronger than ever.

You don't have to prove your worth to yourself or anyone else. Because you are human, you are worthy. There is good inside of you, and there is something that someone will love. You should never have to jump through hoops to prove that you can be a good partner for another person. If someone cannot see your worth right away, then they are not treating you in a way that will ever lead to a secure relationship. You must be in a relationship with a person who sees you as worthwhile right away because if you have to prove it, you'll feel like you have to keep proving it throughout your relationship, and you'll never have peace.

Learn to save yourself rather than wanting someone else to save you. Many people have a fantasy that their partner will save them from their worries. They think, "If I can find the perfect partner for me, I will never worry again." In the process, they push away perfectly good romantic relationships because they are afraid, and they are looking for a partner who doesn't exist. You'll never find a partner who can do everything that makes you feel secure because if they have to go all the way to where you're standing to meet you, they have to forgo some of their autonomy. One partner cannot expect the other partner to automatically give information simply for the sake of patching up their partner's insecurity; such a dynamic wouldn't be a healthy relationship.

No one will be able to give you everything you want to feel secure. For example, some partners wouldn't want to show their partner all their texts because texts are personal, but that doesn't mean those texts have untrustworthy content. Your partner may say no to a request like that, which can make the insecurely attached feel anxious. The issue is that there's always going to be a boundary, as seen in the text scenario, that makes full transparency impossible. In that case, to have a perfect partner, you need to have a robot carefully programmed for your needs. Human relationships require trust, so you have to work on yourself if you want anything to change. Expecting your partner to cater to your insecurities doesn't make the insecurities go away; all it does is delay the anxious feelings. Until you address the roots of your issue, you will be stuck.

If you want to change, you need to start being your own number one cheerleader. Before you try to blame your partner for how you feel, you need to look inwards and take note of your own accountability for the state of your relationship. In most scenarios, you will find that insecurities cause some of the issues in the relationship. Some of your worries may be genuine, and your partner usually has some accountability of their own, but when you don't even consider that you may be part of the problem, you are doing your relationship and yourself a great injustice. Support yourself on this journey, and urge yourself to be more self-aware. Identify what makes you anxious before it ruins a perfectly good relationship.

8

THE SELF ESTEEM, INTIMACY, AUTONOMY SHORTCUT

When you have an insecure attachment style, several questions may linger in your head. How do you stop fixating on what your partner may be doing to worsen the relationship and start focusing on active behaviors you can use to make your relationships feel safer? When you are anxiously attached, how do you be independent while still letting yourself be vulnerable? The answers to these questions are three essential patterns that you must build in yourself if you want to create a more secure attachment style. You must learn to have more self-esteem so that you feel worthy, deepen your ability to create intimacy in relationships, and learn to be more autonomous so that you can stand on your own two feet. These tasks can be hard for people who have an insecure attachment, but they are some of the most important acts of self-improvement that you can accomplish when you are trying to create a more secure attachment style because they force you to focus on what is happening within yourself, and they give you constructive ways to improve those issues.

Self-Esteem

As a child, when a parent doesn't live up to expectations and doesn't meet your needs, you don't associate that failure as a flaw of your parent; rather, you attribute your caregiver's failure as something that was a fault of your own. As you start to attribute more problems to yourself, you may begin to think that there is something inherently wrong with you or that you ruin things. This mindset can follow you into adulthood, and it can result in low self-esteem because you always assume that something must be wrong with you, and that's why problems occur in your life and your loved one's lives. Self-esteem is vital for relationship security because if you have low self-esteem, the same old doubts will repeat in your head and make it hard for you to get close to anyone. When you don't have self-esteem, you don't know how to love yourself, and when you cannot love yourself, it's pretty hard to think that anyone could love you in return (but they can, no matter who you are, there's someone who will and can love you).

Think about the areas that cause you to feel the worst about yourself. These areas might be triggering for you, and they point out your biggest insecurities. Maybe you feel worst about your job. While your job insecurity may feel unrelated to your work insecurity, both of those insecurities can be fueled by the thought that you will never measure up. Insecurities are often caused by parents who instill those feelings in you when you were young. Thus, as you can see, insecurities are commonly multi-dimensional, and they impact various parts of your life. Your boss may scold you for not doing your work as well as you should have; then, you go home, and your partner may only criticize you on something minor, but that comment may make you feel unhinged and unloved because that same feeling of insufficiency is piling up on you. By knowing which areas make you feel the worst, you can start to insulate yourself from the negative feelings that pop up and make you unhappy both with yourself and your relationship.

Accept that you will fail, and that's okay. Wanting to be perfect in a relationship, or anything in life, is a disaster waiting to happen, and it will lead to a lack of confidence because you can never reach perfection. To have self-esteem, you need to acknowledge that failure is part of life and that you cannot shield yourself from ever doing anything wrong. You will disappoint people in your life, and you will disappoint yourself. You will take the wrong path and stumble plenty of times, but in all the hardship, you will learn. Without failure, you can never do better. If you get everything right, you never succeed because part of success is learning to manage the hardships. If something were easy, it wouldn't feel rewarding to complete it. Thus, don't look at failure as an indicator that there's something wrong with you. There's nothing wrong with you; you're just human, and you're exploring the world. You're learning to be a better version of yourself, and that requires you to challenge the parts of yourself that are flawed.

Self-care is vital for self-esteem because it proves your value. When you don't take care of yourself, you send the message that you don't care about your body or your mind. Show yourself that you are worthwhile by treating yourself to love, compassion, and special treats. It's not selfish to give yourself a gift or take time for relaxation. You need to put resources into yourself because you invest in things that make you confident and run away from things you believe will be disasters. Believing that you are an investment will remind you that you have inherent worth, and you can use that worth to create fantastic outcomes. Stop putting yourself last. While altruism is admirable, there are times when you need to take care of yourself before you can care for anyone else.

Indulge your interests. Don't run away from the things you love or call them "weird." Many people don't embrace their passions because they think that other people won't understand them. As long as your passions aren't hurting yourself or other people, there's nothing wrong with them. Take time to do the things you love, even those things that are not hobbies that your partner loves. You're allowed and encouraged to have interests that are all your own. When you allow yourself to indulge your interests, you start to see that the things that make you most happy and passionate are also the things that make you feel most confident.

Challenge your beliefs about yourself. If negative beliefs are stuck in your head, start to interrogate those ideas. Most of them have no real basis. If you keep saying to yourself, "I am ugly," start to challenge what that means. What makes you ugly? Ugly is subjective, so while you may use a societal standard for what you call ugly, you don't have to submit to that standard. If you poke around with your negative thoughts, you'll start to realize that you're not being fair to yourself. In another example, you may think, "My partner will never love me." Again, take time to ask yourself why you think that and see if you can find ways that your thinking is untrue. In most cases, you'll find that the assumptions you are making about yourself and your partner are based on fear and not the truth. For each negative assumption, there are positive ones that you can make.

Stop thinking in terms of what you should do or have to do. Self-esteem relies on a sense of autonomy (more on that later), and you need to pull yourself away from forces that are pressuring you to be someone else. Whether it is work standards, parenting standards, or beauty standards, society loves to set a mold and tell you to form yourself to that mold. Unfortunately, that mold is just an illusion. People are all created differently with diverse DNA and unique experiences, so no one person can be exactly like another. Even identical twins are distinguishable because they may look alike, but they are not the same! Don't let anyone tell you that you should be a certain way because when you give into other people's expectations, you try to force yourself into being something you never can be. No matter how hard you push yourself to be someone else, you can only be yourself, and the more you push to be someone else, the more you feel like a failure as you cannot reach the ideal you strive to become.

Remind yourself that you'll be okay. It may seem like the world is a dark, unpredictable, and chaotic place, and often, it can be all of those things. Nevertheless, there's also a lot of good in the world and good in yourself. You're not a lost cause. No matter how unsure you feel, you are programmed to survive, so while no one likes to endure pain, whatever pain comes your way is something you can handle as long as you're still alive. Don't close yourself off or get combative when you're scared. Learn that if you're rejected, it often has more to do with the other person than it does with you. Sometimes, relationships don't work, and it's no one's fault. Take the lessons you learned from that relationship and move on because it won't feel great, but sooner or later, you're going to feel better.

Know that you are not your thoughts or your feelings. Neither your thoughts nor your feelings define your worth. If you feel sad or angry, that doesn't mean that you are a sad or angry person. Similarly, if you think something bad, that doesn't determine that you are a bad person. What really defines you is your actions. We all have negative thoughts and feel ways we know aren't logical, but we are so much more than those thoughts or feelings. We have the choice to decide what we want to do. Thus, don't base your worth on your thoughts or feelings because if you do that, you will focus on the parts of yourself that you don't like rather than the good ones. When you find yourself letting thoughts and feelings make you feel bad about yourself, think of all the times that you've thought about doing bad things but instead made a choice to do good; those moments tell you that you have value.

Stand up for yourself. Don't listen when other people call you worthless or suggest that you are unlovable. Other people cannot define your worth, and when they try to tear you down, you need to build yourself up. Don't internalize the unwarranted, unconstructive criticisms other people throw your way. Standing up for yourself doesn't always mean you have to confront the other person, though that is an option; it can also mean that you stand firm in your sense of self and don't let the doubts that others create linger for too long in your head. Sometimes, standing up for yourself merely means standing up to the negative bully in your own brain.

Don't just focus on your mental self, but you should also focus on your physical health. While you shouldn't put too much focus on your looks, the way your body feels physically can contribute to increased self-esteem. If you feel good about what your body can do, confidence naturally follows. Adding more exercise into your routine is an ideal way to improve your body. Exercise shouldn't be about changing your body, and it doesn't have to feel like a chore. Even simple activities like walking outside or going for a leisurely swim can make you feel happier and give you a mood boost. When you feel healthy, it functions better, which allows you to do more and be more confident.

Self-esteem is one of the most vital attributes for your overall well-being and your relationships because it represents your relationship with yourself. If you want a healthy relationship with anyone else, you need to learn to respect yourself because if you don't respect yourself, you'll doubt that anyone else will ever give it to you. By becoming more self-aware and starting to take care of yourself better, you will transform your self-esteem. If you have a hard time with this process, remember that you can start with small acts of self-love and build up more self-confidence as you get used to the idea. While arrogance is not a good trait, confidence will change your life and allow you to enter relationships with less insecurity.

Intimacy

Intimacy is one of the most rewarding parts of relationships because it keeps an honest and healthy tie between two people. You can experience intimacy on many levels, and many people associate it with sexual relationships, but it is so much more than a sexually fueled thing. You can have sex that deepened intimacy, but you can also have sex that is never intimate. Thus, intimacy not only refers to sexual relations, but it refers to a connection between two people. It often refers to emotional intimacy more than just physical closeness. Emotional intimacy means that you have deeper closeness in your relationship, and you allow yourself to be vulnerable. Through that vulnerability, you and your partner trust each other more, and you love each other in more reassuring manners. The more you can share with your partner, the better your communication will become. As you create increased intimacy, you will start to see that your relationship grows and it becomes more secure naturally.

One of the best ways to create intimacy is to ask questions because questions help you learn about the other person through their perspective rather than through your biased one. Research shows that certain questions can produce intimacy, even among strangers. Arthur Aaron and his fellow researchers have studied these questions, and they promote people to learn about one another's deepest desires and interests. When you ask these questions, you begin a conversation that allows people to speak their minds without as much fear that you will reject their passions. You open the dialogue and show that you are willing to listen. With your openness, the other person becomes open as well.

Some of these questions you can ask are:

- What possession would you save first if your home were burning?
- What is your relationship with ___ like? (insert family member, best friend, boss, etc.).
- How do you feel about your childhood?
- If you could invite anyone over to dinner, dead or alive, who would it be?

- Can you describe what your ideal day would look like?
- What's the song you sang?
- When you are about to call someone, do you plan what you will say to them?
- If you could go back in time and change one thing about your upbringing, what would you change?
- What are the three things that you think we have the most in common?
- Do you think you know how you will die?
- What are the most important qualities for your friends to have?
- What kind of affection most touches your heart?
- What is your favorite memory?
- What is your worst memory?
- What would you want your future children to know about your life?
- When did you last cry?
- Do you regret saying something or not saying something to anyone?

These questions are just a few that you can ask to spark conversation and facilitate a deeper connection between you and your partner, and as you ask more of these questions, you'll start to understand your partner in new ways.

Learn what your partner's love language is and learn what yours is because these love languages speak to the acts of love that you and your partner should be sharing. A love language is a way that other people feel loved, as dictated by Dr. Gary Chapman. There are five love languages: Quality time, acts of service, receiving gifts, affirmations, and physical touch. When you don't have your love language fulfilled, you will feel neglected and insecure, and when someone has a different love language than you, you may think that you are showing them some love when the love you are showing doesn't translate to the other person.

For people whose love language is quality time, they want their partner to commit time into the relationship, and they don't just want the other person to spend time with them, but they also want undivided attention during that time, so if you're spending time with someone who has this love language, using your phone can make them feel neglected and unwanted, which fuels their anxieties. People who have this love language will often show you their love by actively listening to you and wanting to spend many meaningful moments with you.

Someone with an act of service love language, meanwhile, feels content when their partner makes an effort to do extra things for them, such as taking out the trash or making a fancy dinner. They will show love by doing acts of service too, such as caring for you when you're sick or cleaning the house. They like you to show them how appreciated they are. For this love language, actions speak louder than words, and gratitude for your partner's efforts is crucial because if they feel underappreciated, the insecure loop in their head will begin to play.

Receiving gifts is the third love language that people may have. Some people like to get gifts because gifts are a visual reminder of the other person's dedication. They often show their love by giving little tokens of their appreciation, even when they have no reason to do so. When you are using this love language, you don't need to give your partner expensive gifts. It is most important to find gifts that have meaning and serve as reminders about your relationship. Things that represent inside jokes, flowers or something they've been wanting to get are all ideas of objects that will provide the sensation of love.

Many people also like affirmations in their relationships. People who have this love language want other people's love for them to be stated either through writing, speech, or other forms of communication. They want to hear the words "I love you" and will show their love by telling you those words as well. Further, these people want you to tell them that they are appreciated. Staying in touch with them throughout the day can alleviate the worries they have. When you don't communicate your love, people with this love language will feel heightened anxiety even if you show them their love through things like gifts or acts of service.

Finally, the final love language is physical touch. People with this love language tend to show their love to you by kissing you, hugging you, or giving you other types of physical attention. These people might start to get upset when you haven't cuddled for a while, or you haven't had sex. While both parties need to feel comfortable with physical touch in a relationship, finding touch that makes you both feel good can promote a sense of belonging and care in a person with this love language. Remember consent is still important here, so be sure your partner is okay with whatever you do!

Beyond just trying to understand how your partner gives and receives love, try to break your routines. Trying new things with your partner is a great way to explore the world together and dance the things that make you fearful. When you invest in a new experience with a loved one, you allow yourself to share something special with the other person. Relationships don't do well with stagnancy. Stagnancy may feel safer, but it doesn't allow progress. To further your relationship, you must risk bringing up hard truths. It's better to face those truths than to keep you and your partner from walking together into the future. Change is inevitable, so learn to promote it rather than hiding from it!

Don't forget the good times you've had with the other person, and let yourself be optimistic about the good times that you will have in the future. Remembering the good times you've had with another person makes you more likely to initiate intimacy because it reminds you that you have already established a connection in the past. If you cannot think of any good times between you and another person, you either are shrouded in negativity, or that person is not the right fit for you. In any case, remembering the best parts of your relationships helps you think of the good times you can recreate and use as future inspiration. Maybe you have a hobby you used to do together that you haven't done in a while, or you used to go to a restaurant you both loved. Those good times can continue.

No matter how long you've been with someone, scheduling date nights or weekend trips can help you reconnect because it makes your relationship a priority rather than leaving it to sit on the back burner. When you get busy, you need to make an extra effort to create time for your relationship. Setting weekly time for you to spend with your partner can ensure that you maintain intimacy and repair areas that might cause friction and misunderstanding. If you don't make time for intimacy, you can never be intimate with another person. Everyone has a busy life, but you are never too busy to make time for the people you want to build a connection with. Regular moments of intimacy will reassure anyone who has doubts about their relationships fueled by an insecure attachment style.

Intimacy is created mostly by spending time with one another and attending to each other's physical and emotional needs. You cannot expect intimacy instantly because it takes time and effort to create it between two people. It requires effort from both parties, so you must be on the same page with your partner about the kind of intimacy you want and what you are willing to do to get it. You also have to maintain intimacy. As you progress, continue to check-in with how your intimacy is holding up. While you may build intimacy up to its highest heights, if you don't keep in communication and continue to share information with your partner, the intimacy will begin to crumble. Think of it this way: no matter how grand a building is when people first construct it, it won't stay that way unless you make repairs over time. Thus, intimacy is not a one-time act or something you can ignore once you get it. It will get easier to engage in acts of intimacy over time, and you'll realize that the reward is well worth the work you must put into the relationship.

Autonomy

One of the most important qualities you need to forge secure relationships is autonomy, and when you have the autonomy to what makes you happy, you can also have greater intimacy in relationships because autonomy allows you to embrace yourself and your partner's unique perspectives and roles in the relationship. While autonomy may seem like it is the opposite of intimacy, these two concepts are both important in a secure relationship. You each must give up some autonomy for intimacy, but it is just as important that you feel like you have a distinct sense of self, or you will similarly be unable to be intimate because intimacy requires you to be aware of yourself and your interests.

Autonomy is the idea that you can stand on your own and make your decisions without becoming overly reliant on the opinions or needs of others at the expense of your own. Autonomy helps you create healthy boundaries and preserve your interests.

When you have the agency to be yourself, you can still feel close to people, even when you have been doing things on your own and paying attention to your unique interests. In every relationship, people need room to express themselves and embrace their identities. A relationship that doesn't have autonomy for both parties reaps insecurity because the line between the self and the relationship becomes too blurred.

Don't give up "me" in an attempt to create "we." When you and your partner start sharing more parts of your life, you don't have to sacrifice things that are already important to you. You don't have to be a unit in every area. It's good to be unified and have that "We can do this together" spirit, but there are some things that have to be yours because when you have certain things that are just your own, you don't become too intertwined with another person that losing them could feel like losing yourself. In a relationship, you need to be able to stand on your feet, but you can take turns being the one who is walking, and you don't always have to walk side by side. Don't forget that you're the same person you've always been, and your partner should bring out the best in you without trying to change who you inherently are.

Let your partner see beyond your persona. As Billy Joel says in his song, *The Stranger*, "Did you ever let your lover see the stranger in yourself?" So many people close themselves off to the point that they almost forget that the person they show the world isn't the truest version of themselves. Everyone has parts of themselves that they tend to hide from other people, and these parts stand alone. They are the parts of yourself that you may both love and hate all at once. Don't hide the unique parts of yourself from your partner. It's good to show your partner that there's so much more to you than being in a relationship. When you show your partner more than the image you put into the world, you allow them to know your autonomous side without letting them change it.

It's okay to say no. When your partner wants you to do something that you aren't comfortable with, you don't need to feel pressured just because you are in a relationship. You're still allowed to have your morals and stick to them. If your partner tries to make you change your values, they are not respecting your boundaries, and you should address that lack of respect because if you aren't allowed to have the autonomy you need, the relationship is always going to be fragmented by your insecurities. Compromise when you can, but when you have firm boundaries in place, keep them in place. You can push your boundaries, but don't remove them merely because your partner wants you to do so. Remember that true teamwork isn't about agreeing with other people all the time. You don't have to feel the same way as your partner or think the same. You'll want to act in ways that help both of you, but part of teamwork is talking through the options and finding some middle ground.

Balance the time you spend together and the time you spend apart from your partner. The balance you create is different in each relationship, but you must find one that satisfies both you and your partner. You can't be spending every moment with another person because that's a sure way to lose your autonomy, and it could even lead to codependency. Don't feel guilty for doing things without your partner, and try to allow your partner the same freedom to have their autonomy as well because if you don't let them be autonomous, they may grow resentful.

Create a support system outside of your relationship. While you should be able to talk to your partner about your concerns, it's never healthy to become overdependent on the other person. Make sure that you have friends who will listen to you if you need to get certain things off your chest and who will be there for you if something goes wrong in the relationship. Relationships are always less scary when you know that you'll have at least one person in your corner no matter what. Your social circle needs to be bigger than just your partner because you need that for your health.

Don't try to control your partner. Just as you need autonomy, your partner needs it as well. Relationships are two-sided, and if you cling too tightly to your partner, that causes insecurity in them. Your actions can then cause your partner to push away, which reinforces your insecurities. Thus, when you or your partner doesn't allow the other person to have the space they need, it threatens to create a disastrous chain-reaction that makes everyone unhappy and destroys the relationship (despite your frantic behaviors being in an attempt to save the relationship). You cannot force closeness. For any closeness to be genuine, you have to allow the other person to choose what they want to share with you and decide they want to open up, and your partner must let you decide how you will welcome them into your life as well.

You need to fight for your autonomy because it will make your relationship more enjoyable and less anxiety-inducing. You may be tempted to blend into your partner's interests and to ignore the unusual or unrelatable interests that you have, but if you want to feel confident and secure in your relationship, you have to embrace your agency because everyone is entitled to have their opinions and feelings without needing to censor those things. Censorship may keep the peace, but it doesn't allow your partner to get to know you better. Accordingly, if you cannot be your true self to your partner and feel like you have to stop being autonomous, your relationship can never be intimate, healthy, or secure. When you learn about yourself and your needs as an autonomous human being, you can establish a relationship that kills all your doubts and makes you feel safe.

CONCLUSION

When you have an insecure attachment style, you may have intense anxiety in relationships. You may self-sabotage and inadvertently destroy relationships just as they start to get more serious. It may be hard for you to trust your partner, and you may think that your partner may never love you in the way that you want to be loved. All these insecurities not only make you feel bad about your relationships, but they make you feel bad about yourself. They make you feel on edge, and they prevent you from being mindful.

Before you can heal yourself, you must face your past. You must accept that people might have let you down when you were a child and even into adulthood, but while that seems like the norm, it doesn't have to be. You can fight for relationships that fulfill your needs rather than ones that leave you feeling scared and alone. It takes time and effort to change the negative thinking that holds you back, but you can start right now.

While you may feel stuck with your relationship anxieties, you can start to rewrite your dialogues with yourself and your partner. When you learn to look at situations in new ways, you start to challenge the ideas that are limiting you. By learning to communicate more clearly and expressing your feelings more honestly with the people in your life, you can begin to build vulnerability and trust with another person that you need to feel secure in romantic relationships. You must learn to have more self-esteem, autonomy, and intimacy because these components allow you to understand yourself better and maintain appropriate boundaries within your relationship. You have to feel good about yourself before you can trust a relationship. If you don't think you are worth happiness and love, you'll always worry that your partner doesn't think you are worth it either. By working on yourself just as much as you work on building more open communication with your partner, you will start to remind yourself that those fears you have can feel incredibly scary, but without the risks of closeness, you will never feel happy.

You don't have to continue having an insecure attachment style. By continuing as you are, you are hampering all your relationships. You are stagnating yourself and not letting yourself reach true intimacy. The more you let your anxiety linger, the harder it becomes to challenge the deeply ingrained ideas that it has created. Take the time to build better relationships by treating yourself with more love and mercy. You are not perfect, but you deserve respect and compassion.

This book has given you the tools that you need to start making the changes that will transform your relationships. If you enjoyed this book, please leave a review on Amazon and share how it has helped you grow. Further, share it with other people in your life who may struggle to have a secure attachment style because everyone deserves to have healthy, fulfilling relationships that are free of anxiety.

REFERENCES

Abrams, A. (2017, March 27). 8 Steps to Improving Self-Esteem. Retrieved January 11, 2021, from https://www.psychologytoday.com/us/blog/nurturing-self-compassion/201703/8-steps-improving-you

Ackerman, C. E. (2020, December 9). *What is Attachment Theory? Bowlby's 4 Stages Explained.* PositivePsychology.Com. https://positivepsychology.com/attachment-theory/

American Addiction Centers. (n.d.). *Love and Mental Illness: A Survey of Psychological Well-Being and Intimate Partnerships.* PsychGuides.Com. Retrieved December 8, 2020, from https://www.psychguides.com/interact/love-and-mental-illness/

REFERENCES

Anatomy and physiology of the nervous system - Canadian Cancer Society. (n.d.). Retrieved December 23, 2020, from https://www.cancer.ca/en/cancer-information/cancer-type/neuroblastoma/neuroblastoma/the-nervous-system/?region=on

Apodaca, M. (2018, July 6). Striving Towards Secure Attachment: How to Restructure Your Thoughts. Retrieved January 5, 2021, from https://www.lifehack-.org/788867/secure-attachment

Bailey, K. (2018, November 15). 5 Powerful Health Benefits of Journaling. Retrieved January 5, 2021, from https://intermountainhealthcare.org/blogs/topics/live-well/2018/07/5-powerful-health-benefits-of-journaling/

Bhatia, M. (2017, September 4). *The Importance of Appreciation in a Relationship.* HuffPost. https://www.huffpost.com/entry/the-importance-of-appreciation-in-a-relationship_b_59ad1b54e4b0d0c16bb52671

Bhatia, M. (2017, September 4). *The Importance of Appreciation in a Relationship.* HuffPost. https://www.huffpost.com/entry/the-importance-of-appreciation-in-a-relationship_b_59ad1b54e4b0d0c16bb52671

Bowden, D. (2020, September 23). 19 Eye-Opening Social Media and Self Esteem Statistics. Retrieved January 5, 2021, from https://www.irreverentgent.com/social-media-and-self-esteem-statistics/

Brady, K. (2020, September 9). 10 Ways To Increase Intimacy In Your Relationship. Retrieved January 13, 2021, from http://www.keirbradycounseling.com/10-ways-to-increase-intimacy/

Broadwater, A. (2020, October 9). 9 Pieces of Relationship Advice for People With an Anxious Attachment Style. Retrieved January 13, 2021, from https://goodmenproject.com/featured-content/9-pieces-of-relationship-advice-for-people-with-an-anxious-attachment-style/

Brogaard, B. (2015, March 18). How to Change Your Attachment Style. Retrieved January 11, 2021, from https://www.psychologytoday.com/us/blog/the-mysteries-love/201503/how-change-your-attachment-style

Cafasso, J. (2019, November 14). *What Is Anxious Attachment?* Healthline. https://www.healthline.com/health/mental-health/anxious-attachment

Calming the Anxious Attachment Style. (2018, September 21). Retrieved January 13, 2021, from https://www.thehappinessclinic.org/single-post/calming-the-anxious-attachment-style

Carlos, V. (2016, February 22). *The Science Of Adult Attachment: Are You Anxious, Avoidant Or Secure?* Elite Daily. https://www.elitedaily.com/dating/science-attachment-styles/1378133

Cleaveland Clinic. (n.d.). *Reactive Attachment Disorder: Causes, Symptoms & Treatment.* Cleveland Clinic. Retrieved December 14, 2020, from https://my.clevelandclinic.org/health/diseases/17904-reactive-attachment-disorder

Cutlip, M. (2017, August 26). *How to meet your partner's needs in 3 easy steps.* My Love Thinks. https://mylovethinks.com/meet-your-partners-needs/

Cherry, K. (2020, August 4). What You Should Know About Attachment Styles. Retrieved December 23, 2020, from https://www.verywellmind.com/attachment-styles-2795344

Communication Exercises for Couples Who Cannot Afford Counseling. (n.d.). Retrieved January 5, 2021, from https://hellorelish.com/articles/free-communication-exercises-for-couples.html

CrashCourse. (2015, March 23). *Central Nervous System: Crash Course A&P #11* [Video file]. Retrieved from https://www.youtube.com/watch?v=q8NtmDrb_qo&feature=youtu.be

Cuncic, A. (2020, December 23). Tips to Help You Date More Mindfully. Retrieved January 5, 2021, from https://www.verywellmind.com/mindful-dating-4177839

Dail, R., & Howard, J. (2018, September 20). The Mindset Mentor - How Your Brain Affects Your Relationships. Retrieved

December 23, 2020, from https://podcasts.google.com/feed/aHR0cHM6Ly9yc3MuYXJ0MTkuY29tL3RoZS1taW5kc2V0LW1lbnRvcg/episode/NjZlZmRlYTBlNTAyNGMyMWJlYmJhYzc4OThjZDc0NjU?sa=X&ved=2ahUKEwjxutzvgZXrAhXxazABHcPhADwQkfYCegQIARAG

Ellis E.E., Yilanli M, Saadabadi A. Reactive Attachment Disorder. (Updated 2020 Nov 19). In: StatPearls. Treasure Island (FL): StatPearls Publishing. January 2020, from https://www.ncbi.nlm.nih.gov/books/NBK537155/

Emily, J. (2020, July 29). 15 Powerful Communication Exercises For Couples To Grow Closer. Retrieved January 5, 2021, from https://defeatingdivorce.com/communication-exercises-for-couples/

familyeducation.com. (2019, July 11). Use Positive Reinforcement. Retrieved December 23, 2020, from https://www.familyeducation.com/life/positive-reinforcement/use-positive-reinforcement

Farley, R. C. (2018). *A Brief Overview of Adult Attachment Theory and Research*. R. Chris Farley. http://labs.psychology.illinois.edu/%7Ercfraley/attachment.htm

Firestone, L. (2017, June 28). How Embracing Vulnerability Strengthens Our Relationships. Retrieved January 5, 2021, from https://www.psychalive.org/embracing-vulnerability-strengthens-connections/

Gage, F. H. (2015). Neuroscience: The Study of the Nervous System & Its Functions. Retrieved December 23, 2020, from https://www.amacad.org/publication/neuroscience-study-nervous-system-its-functions

Gaultiere, B. (2016, September 5). Secure and Insecure Attachment Styles. Retrieved December 23, 2020, from https://www.soulshepherding.org/secure-insecure-attachment-styles/

Gray, J. (2020, April 26). 6 Exercises For Couples To Build Intimacy. Retrieved January 5, 2021, from https://www.jordangrayconsulting.com/6-connection-exercises-for-couples-to-build-intimacy/Hanson, R. (2018, November 19). Intimacy and Autonomy. Retrieved January 13, 2021, from https://www.rickhanson.net/intimacy-and-autonomy/

Hempstead, K. (n.d.). *How our Attachment Styles might be Ruining our Relationships.* Kevin Hempsted Counselling. Retrieved December 17, 2020, from https://kevinhempstedcounsellor.com/articles/f/how-our-attachment-styles-might-be-ruining-our-relationships

Hopper, E. (2017, September 19). *Can You Cultivate a More Secure Attachment Style?* Greater Good. https://greatergood.berkeley.edu/article/item/can_you_cultivate_a_more_secure_attachment_style

How Can I Improve My Self-Esteem? (for Teens) - Nemours KidsHealth. (n.d.). Retrieved January 13, 2021, from https://kidshealth.org/en/teens/self-esteem.html

Hutchinson, T. (2019, February 22). *Why are Personal Boundaries Important? Your Rights in a Relationship.* Tracy Hutchinson, PhD | Fort Myers Therapy. https://www.drtracy-hutchinson.com/what-are-personal-boundaries-and-why-are-they-important/

Intimacy Exercises For Couples: 7 Ways To Build Feelings Of Connection, Trust And Love | Regain. (2019, October 4). Retrieved January 11, 2021, from https://www.regain.us/advice/intimacy/intimacy-exercises-for-couples-7-ways-to-build-feelings-of-connection-trust-and-love/

Jones, D. (2019, January 11). The 36 Questions That Lead to Love. Retrieved January 13, 2021, from https://www.nytimes.com/2015/01/09/style/no-37-big-wedding-or-small.html

Kahneman, D. (2013). *Thinking, Fast and Slow* [Kindle] (1st ed.). Retrieved fromMy Book

Kämmerer, A. (2019, August 9). The Scientific Underpinnings and Impacts of Shame. Retrieved January 5, 2021, from https://www.scientificamerican.com/article/the-scientific-underpinnings-and-impacts-of-shame/

Kandola, A. (2020, November 2). *What is reactive attachment disorder?* Medical News Today. https://www.

medicalnewstoday.com/articles/reactive-attachment-disorder#in-adolescents-and-adults

Lee, A., & Hankin, B. L. (2009). Insecure Attachment, Dysfunctional Attitudes, and Low Self-Esteem Predicting Prospective Symptoms of Depression and Anxiety During Adolescence. *Journal of Clinical Child Adolescent Psychology*, 219–231. https://doi.org/10.1080/15374410802698396

Lee, J. (2020, April 8). *Anxious Attachments in Relationships*. ACEsConnection. https://www.acesconnection.com/blog/anxious-attachments-in-relationships

Lindberg, S. (2018, July 25). How to Forgive Yourself. Retrieved January 5, 2021, from https://www.healthline.com/health/how-to-forgive-yourself

Miguel, M. (2020, December 14). *Reactive Attachment Disorder in Adults Ruins Relationships*. The Mighty. https://themighty.com/2019/08/reactive-attachment-disorder-symptoms/

mindbodygreen. (2020, March 2). How To Rewire Your Brain To Have A Secure Attachment Style. Retrieved January 13, 2021, from https://www.mindbodygreen.com/articles/how-to-develop-a-secure-attachment-style

Morris, S. Y. (2016, December 19). What Are the Benefits of Self-Talk? Retrieved January 5, 2021, from https://www.healthline.com/health/mental-health/self-talk#why-it-matters

Nunez, K. (2020, April 18). What Is the ABC Model in Cognitive Behavioral Therapy? Retrieved January 5, 2021, from https://www.healthline.com/health/abc-model

PAIRS Foundation. (n.d.). Relationship Building Exercises for Dating Couples. Retrieved January 5, 2021, from http://www.pairs.com/toolkits/dating

Perry, S. K. (2016, February 19). 10 Proven Ways You Can Increase Intimacy. Retrieved January 13, 2021, from https://www.psychologytoday.com/us/blog/creating-in-flow/201602/10-proven-ways-you-can-increase-intimacy

Peterman, M. (n.d.). 15 Statistics That Prove the Power of Data Visualization. Retrieved January 13, 2021, from https://blog.csgsolutions.com/15-statistics-prove-power-data-visualization

Physical health and mental health. (2020, February 10). Retrieved December 23, 2020, from https://www.mental-health.org.uk/a-to-z/p/physical-health-and-mental-health

Psychology Consultants, Inc. (n.d.). 8 Reasons to Seek Psychological Services. Retrieved January 5, 2021, from https://www.psychologyconsultantsinc.com/8-reasons-to-seek-psychological-services

Psycom.net. (2018, November 18). *Reactive Attachment Disorder: Causes, Symptoms and Treatment.* https://www.psycom.net/reactive-attachment-disorder

Rosen, H.M "Seeking Self-Certainty in an Uncertain Time: Attachment Style and Self-Esteem in Emerging Adulthood" (2016). Student Works. 10. https://commons.clarku.edu/studentworks/10

Sack, D. (2015, January 15). Five Ways to Silence Shame. Retrieved January 5, 2021, from https://www.psychologytoday.com/us/blog/where-science-meets-the-steps/201501/5-ways-silence-shame

Self-esteem: Take steps to feel better about yourself. (2020, July 14). Retrieved January 13, 2021, from https://www.mayoclinic.org/healthy-lifestyle/adult-health/in-depth/self-esteem/art-20045374

Shorley, H. (2015, July 7). Rewiring Your Avoidant, Anxious, or Fearful Attachment Style. Retrieved January 13, 2021, from https://www.psychologytoday.com/us/blog/the-freedom-change/201805/rewiring-your-avoidant-anxious-or-fearful-attachment-style

Simpson, J. A. (2017, February 1). *Adult attachment, stress, and romantic relationships.* ScienceDirect. https://linkinghub.elsevier.com/retrieve/pii/S2352250X16300306

Smith, E. J. (2014, October 27). *Supporting Your Spouse's Interests (Even the Ones that Bug You).* Engaged Marriage. https://www.engagedmarriage.com/supporting-your-spouses-interests-even-the-ones-that-bug-you/

Sparks, C. (2020, December 11). How Early Attachment Styles Can Influence Later Relationships. Retrieved December 23, 2020, from https://www.gottman.com/blog/how-early-attachment-styles-can-influence-later-relationships/

Spears, K. (2018, May 17). Ways To Create A Secure Attachment | Betterhelp. Retrieved from https://www.betterhelp.com/advice/attachment/ways-to-create-a-secure-attachment/

Stanborough, R. (2020, February 4). How to Change Negative Thinking with Cognitive Restructuring. Retrieved January 5, 2021, from https://www.healthline.com/health/cognitive-restructuring#doing-a-cost-benefit-analysis

Steber, C. (2017, December 7). *15 Little Ways To Get Your Partner To Better Understand You Emotionally.* Bustle. https://www.bustle.com/p/15-little-ways-to-get-your-partner-to-better-understand-you-emotionally-7380392

Theida, K. (2014, August 12). *Brene Brown on Empathy vs Sympathy.* Psychology Today. https://www.psychologytoday.com/us/blog/partnering-in-mental-health/201408/bren-brown-empathy-vs-sympathy-0

Trust exercises to try with your partner. (2020, September 28). Retrieved January 5, 2021, from https://www.loveisrespect.org/resources/trust-exercises-to-try-with-your-partner/

UMatter. (n.d.). Autonomy. Retrieved January 11, 2021, from https://umatter.princeton.edu/respect/relationships/autonomy

UNC-Chapel Hill Learning Center. (2020, December 14). Changing Habits –. Retrieved December 23, 2020, from https://learningcenter.unc.edu/tips-and-tools/changing-habits/

University of Toledo Counseling Center. (n.d.). Autonomy and Intimacy. Retrieved January 13, 2021, from https://www.utoledo.edu/studentaffairs/counseling/bridge/autonomy-and-intimacy.html

Village Behavioral Health Treatment Center. (2019, May 15). *Causes, Symptoms & Effects of Attachment Disorders.* Village Behavioral Health. https://www.villagebh.com/disorders/reactive-attachment/symptoms-signs-effects/

What Is the Mind-Body Connection? (n.d.). Retrieved December 23, 2020, from https://www.takingcharge.csh.umn.edu/what-is-the-mind-body-connection

Whittaker, S. (2020, November 5). *155 Dating Statistics [2019] – The Ultimate List of Dating Studies.* Mantelligence. https://www.mantelligence.com/dating-statistics/

wikiHow. (2020, November 18). *How to Date Someone with an Anxious Attachment Style.* https://www.wikihow.com/Date-Someone-with-an-Anxious-Attachment-Style#/Image:Think-of-Stuff-to-Talk-About-with-Your-Boyfriend-Step-3-Version-3.jpg

Wu, J. (2020, April 3). 3 Ways to Overcome Insecure Attachment in Relationships. Retrieved January 13, 2021, from https://www.quickanddirtytips.com/health-fitness/mental-health/overcome-insecure-attachment

Youth Care Treatment Center. (2019, March 29). *Causes and Effects of Reactive Attachment Disorder.* Youthcare. https://www.youthcare.com/behavioral-health/reactive-attachment/signs-symptoms/

Zandijcke, V. M. (2001, March 1). THE NERVOUS SYSTEM AND THE HEART. Edited by Gert J. Ter Horst. 1999. New Jersey: Humana Press. Price $145. Pp. 584. ISBN 0-89603-693-6. Retrieved December 23, 2020, from https://academic.oup.com/brain/article/124/3/637/334403

Printed in Great Britain
by Amazon